Praise for *Landscapes of the Hea*

Beautifully written. An enlightening and helpful exploration of various methodologies brought vividly alive with valuable case study examples that show how couples can recover the closeness of their early relationships whilst, at the same time, developing a deeper and more substantial understanding of each other that leads to a richer partnership. A compelling and lively read, steeped in humanity and compassion. I found her great many insights into the relatively new methodology of Pesso Boyden System Psychomotor fascinating.
Sue Parker Hall, Relational Psychotherapist and Author of
Anger, Rage and Relationship: An Empathic Approach to Anger
Management

Juliet is a skilled therapist who combines an intuitive understanding of relationships with a sound grasp of couples therapy techniques. Her enthusiasm for solving relationship problems, which shines through the text, together with examples of her work, makes this a valuable book for anyone curious about this field of therapy.
Dr Michael Crowe, DM, FRCPsych

Beautifully written and thought provoking, drawing from experience, casework and theory. An outstanding resource for clients and therapists alike. Highly recommended.
Dana Braithwaite, UKCP Registered Psychosexual Therapist

I am delighted to see Juliet publish the first book in the UK describing the effectiveness of Pesso Boyden System Psychomotor (PBSP) in individual and group sessions. This continues Juliet's passion: to spread the message that PBSP is a transformative method that supports people becoming more fully who they truly are and finding greater meaning and pleasure in life.
Al Pesso, Co-Founder of PBSP

This book combines Juliet Grayson's expertise as a couples therapist with the wisdom she has acquired from Pesso Boyden System Psychomotor therapy. By showing how childhood issues come up in couple conflicts and providing resolutions through Pesso Boyden 'antidotes', she breaks new ground.
Barbara Fischer Bartlemann, Dipl. Psych. MA,
Pesso Boyden Trainer

As a lay person, I found Juliet's description of the therapeutic process clear and insightful. Her book gives the reader a strong sense of the power of these approaches, bringing the theoretical material vividly to life.
Dr Sarah Goode, Sociologist and Author

After twenty-five years of dedication to the field of therapy, Juliet shares thoughtful and creative insights into how our lives can change. I've seen her consistent love and support for many people as a therapist, now we get to take that home with us in her writing. Pesso Boyden therapy has an understanding of the unconscious born from Martha Graham dance, and insight into human nature. Juliet is a pioneer of this method in the UK, and I watch her develop it with deep respect.
Marie-Elsa Bragg, Director of Westminster Leadership Consultancy and Duty Chaplain, Westminster Abbey

An accessible and warming read! This book is ideal for one curious about psychotherapy. The style of writing invites a reader to 'sit beside' Juliet – with her clear mind and warm heart – while she finds a way to help and heal her client.
Sandy Cotter, Founding Director of the Praxis Centre at Cranfield School of Management

Landscapes of the Heart can be read from several perspectives. Its easy-to-read style will inform struggling couples – as well as benefit couples who want to improve a satisfactory relationship. Therapists (or anyone interested in becoming a therapist) will

learn about the systemic nature of working with couples from the comprehensive client cases. This is an absorbing, practical and beautifully written book we will recommend to many people.
Penny Tompkins and James Lawley, Authors of
Metaphors in Mind: Transformation through Symbolic Modelling

This is an exciting and interesting book. It explores simply, clearly and sensitively difficulties we have in sexual relationships. Her description of the theoretical context to her work is lucid and accessible, which makes this book a good read for lay readers and practitioners alike.
Jason Wright, MA, UKCP Registered Psychoanalytic
Psychotherapist, Clinical Director of Number 42

It's illuminating to see how the Pesso Boyden System Psychomotor method is applied in Juliet Grayson's compelling account of her work as a relationship and individual therapist.
Sally Potter, Relationship Therapist,
Executive Coach and Accredited Pesso Boyden Trainer

Juliet's book is impressive. She starts off with practical clinical examples that demonstrate her work, and links that to her psychological understanding about human existence.
Lowijs Perquin MD, Psychiatrist

I LOVED IT. Juliet allows us into her therapy room with openness, honesty and passion. The book demystifies couples therapy; it demonstrates how relationships can break down but more importantly how a couple can be helped to put things right again. Congratulations Juliet you have filled a real gap on the bookshelves.
Trudy Hannington, UKCP Registered Psychosexual Therapist

This is an essential read for clients who want to enhance their self-awareness and emotional intelligence.
Judith Lowe, MD of PPD Learning Ltd, NLP Institute, London

Juliet has the ability to enthrall with her narrative. Within a few lines, I was gripped as if reading a page-turning thriller, wanting to know what happened next. It's more than just observational psychology, it's compelling and enlightening. The descriptions of the characters and their relationships are interwoven with Juliet's insights in a dance that carries you along.

Antony Haynes, Registered Nutritional Therapist, Director of The Nutrition Clinic Ltd, Lecturer, Author

Juliet's book is a real jewel. She brings depth and clarity to complex relationship issues in a way that will be of enormous value both to couples themselves as well as to therapists interested in going beyond a 'talking' approach.

Nicholas Janni, Author and Founder of Core Presence

Have you ever been stuck, thought about going to therapy and hesitated? This is a compelling and inspiring book that I feel certain will help anyone interested in improving their relationships.

Sharon Rooke, Psychotherapist, Chair of NLPtCA

Juliet demonstrates a clear theoretical basis for her work, which is well explained. She then uses her creativity, humanity and wisdom to individualise her work and apply it to specific difficulties.

Ruth Hallam Jones, Psychosexual Therapist

A wonderful book. Practical, clearly written and full of insight, it is a valuable contribution to the literature on working with couples.

Robin Shohet, Author and Psychotherapist

Juliet Grayson is an inspirational therapist and teacher. This book is an invaluable contribution that will improve relationships – your own, or other people's. Having witnessed the Pesso Boyden technique myself, I am deeply impressed with this method.

Paula Hall, Sexual & Relationship Psychotherapist, UKCP Reg, BACP Acc Sex Addiction Therapist

Landscapes of the Heart

The Working World of a
Sex and Relationship Therapist

Juliet Grayson

Jessica Kingsley *Publishers*
London and Philadelphia

First published in paperback edition by Sleeping Mountain Press in 2016

This edition first published in 2016

by Jessica Kingsley Publishers

73 Collier Street

London N1 9BE, UK

and

400 Market Street, Suite 400

Philadelphia, PA 19106, USA

www.jkp.com

Copyright © Juliet Grayson 2016

Foreword copyright © Brigid Proctor 2016

Front cover image source: Tavarua Island in Fiji, photograph © musicman, courtesy of Shutterstock®.

Library of Congress Cataloging in Publication Data

A CIP catalog record for this book is available from the Library of Congress

British Library Cataloguing in Publication Data

A CIP catalogue record for this book is available from the B ritish Library

ISBN 978 1 78592 186 5

eISBN 978 1 78450 457 1

Printed digitally in Great Britain and in the Unites States

To my husband, William Ayot

and to

Pia Isabella Christensen Diaz
whose joys and heartaches are yet to come.

Disclaimer

There is a tradition in psychotherapeutic writing in which authors change names and identifying features as a means of protecting the identities and development of clients. My writing follows this tradition and further, alters timing and events for the same purposes.

Acknowledgements

My first thanks must go to my husband, lover, supporter, advisor and best friend, William Ayot. To have found such a gentle love is a true blessing. Without his encouragement to write this book – he started gently pushing me some fifteen years ago – I would never have taken this step. I also want to thank him for introducing me to Pesso Boyden System Psychomotor (PBSP) – a philosophy and a methodology that I truly love. And of course, I want to thank him for the poems.

Other people to thank are: first and foremost my clients, who have taught me so much. My early therapists, Frank Kevlin and Roger Linden. Working with them was truly life changing for me. Two special supervisors: Brigid Proctor – who helped me to combine my integrative counselling training with my NLP, and Mark Kirwin. Ruth Hallam Jones, who so generously passed on her knowledge and mentored me, and Mary Clegg – my colleague, fellow trainer and accomplished couples therapist, who kindly checked the medical aspects of the book. Ram Dass, Ramana Maharshi, Jean Klein, the Dhamma Dipa Vipassana Meditation Centre and the Lam Rim Buddhist Centre have all been really important.

Huge thanks and appreciation go to Al Pesso and his wife Diane Boyden-Pesso for creating this wonderful method, and specifically to Al for his always enthusiastic teaching and role modelling. I feel immense gratitude towards Lowijs Perquin, who has had endless patience, steadfastly supporting me, encouraging me, and assisting my growth since 2001, as he helped me to learn the intricacies of

PBSP. Thanks to Barbara Fischer Bartelmann for her encouragement and support with all the technical detail. I feel a huge appreciation for the colleagues and friends who have shared my PBSP journey from the start: Sally Potter for her love, precision and care, and Sandy Cotter for her wisdom about bodies – both fellow co-trainers in PBSP. Also Pete Mann, Jon Chapman and Kate Lowry, who have been with me through the PBSP journey.

From other areas: the names that stand out from NLP are: Judith Lowe above all, Julian Russell, Robert Dilts, Christina Hall, Judith DeLozier, and Stephen Gilligan. Murray Bowen, David Schnarch and his wife Ruth Morehouse for their ideas and theories on emotional fusion that changed my life. Sue Parker Hall for her wonderful work on anger and rage. Barbara Turner-Vesselago, who has helped me change the way I write. My brother, Nicholas Pearce, for brotherly kindness, and my parents who taught me so much about relationships.

Finally, I thank Sarah Bird, for supporting me, for giving me a chance and for the encouragement to actually start writing this book. Her careful and loving editing has vastly improved it! Thanks are due to Jane Walsh for her tireless reading and support of the first drafts and Carolyn Waterstone who solidly supported me in many ways. Thanks too to others who have directly contributed: Adrien Ferrabee, Ana Diaz, Andrew Christensen, Alison Kerruish, Antony Haynes, Brigid Proctor, Caroline Methven, Craig Smith, Dana Braithwaite, Denis Kennedy, Denise Shepherd, Ellie Hemingway, Florencia Clifford, James Lawley, Janie Dixon, Jan Ross, Jason Wright, Joanna Reader, John Browning, Jonnie Godfrey, Kate Reynolds, Kay Russell, Kirstie Adamson, Libby Lee, Marie-Elsa Bragg, Dr Michael Crowe, Nicholas Janni, Paula Hall, Penny Tompkins, Rachel Dickens, Robin Shohet, Rose Swales, Rosie Godfrey, Sarah Goode, Sharon Rooke, Trudy Hannington, Wayne Sercombe. All have helped and encouraged me by reading, guiding, shaping and praising this book.

Foreword
by Brigid Proctor

I am sure that anyone reading this book will find it a good read and I hope it will reach a wide range of readers.

It was originally written for those who may be interested in going for help and counselling for their partner relationship. However it will also, I am sure, be of interest to counsellors, therapists and psychologists who work mainly one-to-one, giving them the chance to experience a couples therapist at work. Other relationship counsellors, too, will be interested in experiencing the author's 'model' of working, as it offers them a rare chance to compare their own methods. Finally, it is a fascinating read for anyone who is, has been, or hopes to be, in a satisfying core relationship.

The complexity of what happens in counselling and therapy is hard to convey. Here the author offers an acute description of interactions between herself and both of the partners as they engage in couples counselling/therapy. This includes her own unspoken inner dialogue. She then 'steps back' from her description and shares with the reader her understanding, thinking and intention in the session. It is almost as if she runs a video and then comments on it. The result is a wholistic impression of how a therapist feels, experiences, thinks and decides what to do and say.

The book reminds us of the complexity, skilfulness and development that is present, to a greater or lesser extent, in all core relationships that are satisfying and fulfilling to both partners. It also gives careful and generous tips and advice on how to develop relationship skills. It offers reminders of the ages and stages of individual and 'twosome' systems and the challenge of achieving balance at different stages.

Many of the clients who feature in the sessions have never been enabled to develop those skills adequately. The complete absence of any judgmental attitude towards them by the therapist is, in itself, healing and enabling.

The book is a tribute to the skill and wisdom that the author has developed through working (and training others to work) with couples. Her subsequent work with abused and abusive partners could not be more needed.

Brigid Proctor
Founding Member and Fellow of BACP

Contents

Between Dream and Action

And who betrayed you?
Who rose up darkly between dream and action
to comfort and stab with equal aplomb?

Did you see the signs?
Did you read the language, of eyebrow and shoulder,
of significant look and dismissive wave,
the unwitting giveaway in a shrug or a sneer,
        and the dull, lizard eyes behind the smile?

Or was it you who betrayed yourself
with your restless hunger and second-hand certainties?
Maybe you were ambushed by your need to be loved,
or your seeping-cynical view of the world?

What betrays us is the insistent past
which demands that we play out its family fugue —
statement, restatement, in endless repetition,
translating a wound into a way of life.

The past, we can be sure, plays both major and minor.
We may not choose to notice, but it's always there.

William Ayot

Chapter 1

Jamie and Meg

It starts with integrity: telling myself the truth. Then it's about being honest: and telling you the truth too.

J amie was on the trip of a lifetime: flying to India. He ignored the part of him that had always longed to share this trip with the woman of his dreams. He had learnt to shut that off, put it aside. Most of the time at least. But every now and then that feeling would surface. A deep despondency, a heavy weight that sat in the middle of his chest, and a churning in his stomach that reminded him that no one wanted him. That he was alone. And had been for three years now. He didn't really understand it. The way he saw himself, he was an honourable man, kind and always willing to help others.

Meg was small, mousy and timid. Though she had always wanted to go to Delhi, it was really her friend Clare who had pushed her into doing this. It was a big adventure, but her luggage was full of sanitising hand lotion, antibacterial creams, and antiseptic wipes. She hadn't told Clare, but she had brought a box of disposable plastic gloves, which she intended to use in every toilet she visited.

Time to board the plane. As she found her seat, Meg noticed the good-looking man sitting next to her. He had floppy brown hair, a kind face – a bit too thin, with small hands that were almost manicured. She loved his hands, and found herself sneaking a look at them when she could. And that was how they met. By the end of the flight she had found out that he lived alone, only 30 miles away from her. He had a cat, Monty. There was an air of sadness surrounding him, and she wanted to mother him, to feed him up. She laughed as she hadn't for years. She felt so relaxed that before the food had been served she offered him some sanitising hand lotion, and he had used it and didn't seem to think it was odd.

Jamie was sorry that he wasn't spending a night in Delhi – he wanted to see more of Meg. He loved her gentleness, her kindness, and her ready laugh. Normally shy, he plucked up his courage and asked her for her phone number while they were waiting for their luggage. The way she blushed made him like her even more. He was shocked to realise that he was already imagining this woman in his house, picturing her there when he came home from work, pleased to see him. The idea relaxed him.

And so, on their return from India, their relationship had begun. Jamie felt surprisingly confident with Meg. There was something about her delicate gentleness that he found very endearing, and he felt strong when he was with her, in a way that he hadn't with other girlfriends. Many of their friends said that they were the perfect match.

Their lovemaking had followed the same pattern, tentative, each one wanting to please the other. Meg sensed that Jamie was a bit unsure, and she instinctively wanted to protect him, reassure him. In her quiet way, she let him know that he was a good lover, making little noises of pleasure. Most of them were genuine. She realised, with surprise, that she was more experienced than he was – more confident in bed. So, she held that back, reined in her exuberance, and concentrated on him and his pleasure.

Two years on, and the relationship that had seemed so promising had begun to fade. They didn't really talk any more. Meg no longer found herself laughing. It wasn't that they argued – they didn't. It was just that the spark had gone. And that was when they came to see me.

"What do you want from these sessions?" I ask.

"I don't know what is going wrong," Jamie looks at Meg, who looks back at him. Then he begins. "It all started out so well, and I still feel the same about Meggie, but something isn't right. Rather than leave it to go on and on, and then split, we decided to come and see you. We hope that you can tell us what is going wrong, and get us on the right track again."

Implied in Jamie's words is the hope that I will be able to sort it out for them, diagnose the problem and put them right. I wonder if he is going to be willing to do the work that will be needed. I feel both the honour – that he is trusting me with their relationship, and the burden – that he assumes that I am the expert who will sort it out. I don't say anything at this stage, but wonder if he has a habit of giving his power away.

"How do you see it, Meg?" I ask.

She hesitates, and seems nervous. "Well… Jamie is right." She falters, then continues. "We started off so well, and now it feels kind of dead." A silence hangs in the air.

Jamie jumps in. "We still both love each other very much." His voice sounds certain, though I notice he looks questioningly at Meg when he says it, as if wondering if it is *still* true. She pauses, nods, and I notice that he breathes out. *He's relieved,* I think. He's responded so quickly that I wonder if Jamie is uncomfortable with the silence.

Something I find invaluable when working with couples is the pre-therapy form that I send to them. They fill it in separately, and I ask them not to share it. They return it before the first session, and I hope that they can be honest on the form, and don't feel the need to be 'careful' about what they say. There are four pages of questions, ranging from their contact details and information about their doctor, details of their school life and how much they enjoyed it, qualifications, working life, their family of origin, previous relationships, major life events, and what they see as the problem that brings them to therapy. I am intrigued when there are big discrepancies on the form (on one occasion a man mentioned two of his children but forgot to mention the third. In another instance, a woman thought she had been in the relationship for seven years but her husband said it was eleven).

On the pre-therapy form, Jamie and Meg had both said that the relationship was flat, dull and had lost its sparkle. However, Meg had mentioned that the sexual side had never been satisfying, and Jamie hadn't mentioned that. I would need to bring that up later if they didn't raise it themselves.

Meg seems shy and nervous, and I wonder how much of that is being here 'in therapy' for the first time, how much is her natural style, and how much is a learned way of being. There is something about her raising the sexual issue on the form that I had logged. Generally, when sex is mentioned on the form, they both mention it is not good, or that sex is not happening at all. I hypothesise that her mentioning it shows a high level of frustration, or that she finds it difficult to talk about sex in this relationship. At all times, but especially in the first session, I am hoping to tune in to little clues and hunches, tiny indications and whispers that might reveal some truth that isn't spoken. I watch, carefully, to see minute responses that indicate acceptance, or disagreement with what the partner says.

One of my ways of working is to see if I can step into my client's world and feel what it would be like to live there. I inhabit their being for a moment, moving a part of myself over, as if I am stepping into their experience for a very short time.

If I have the history that Meg has (reading the form she sent in has given the bare bones of her history), *if I live in this body* (meaning Meg's body), *if I have these mannerisms, and this way of speaking, how do I feel right now, as Meg? What is going on for me?*

What do I believe about the world? Then, continuing to think and feel as Meg: *what is happening in my body, what do I feel about what Jamie is saying, and the way that Jamie is saying it?*

Then I come back into myself. I might tentatively offer an insight or a thought. I don't assume I have got it quite right, but I offer it to see which bits fit and which don't.

I do the same with Jamie too – feel inside his skin, into what is happening for him, where he feels confident and where he feels misunderstood or not seen. I check. *As Jamie, what is happening in my body? How am I reacting to Meg and what she says? How do I feel about Juliet, and what she is saying?* Then I come back to myself, to Juliet.

When I do this with Meg, I feel something that surprises me. I am more confident inside Meg, stronger when I am in her body than I expected to feel. As Juliet, looking at Meg, I see a shy, nervous, self-effacing mousy woman. When I step in, I experience a kind of steel, a determination and a certainty. *Golly!* I think. Yet it feels too soon to name that, to speak it out loud. They have only been with me for ten minutes.

When working with clients I can only speak as much truth to them as my relationship with them is strong enough to hold. Our rapport forms the container, which has to be resilient enough to handle directness and honesty. If I say too much too soon I can scare them off. They may literally leave and not come back. So I balance the amount of directness and the level of truth-speaking against the strength of our relationship. I never lie to a client, but I might not reveal all of my thinking, until I sense that they can handle hearing it, even if they don't like it! With this couple I think, *I might be able to say something in ten or twenty minutes time, when they trust me a little bit more, and then I will not hold back.* I owe it to them to speak the unspeakable parts. I am concerned that if, right now, I share what I seem to be picking up about her, that there is an inner strength that she is not yet revealing, then I might expose Meg. *It is possible that in the two years that they have been together,* I think, *that Meg has never shown this part of herself directly to Jamie, and it may be too much to tell him just now.* I decide to wait.

The session continues, and as time passes I wonder how honest they are with one another. It feels like there is a kind of politeness in the room, and that they don't quite dare to tell the other one how it really is. This ties in with my feeling that Meg is holding back.

"How honest do you feel you are with one another?" I enquire.

"We can talk about pretty much anything," Jamie responds, but as I hop into Jamie's skin to sense what is going on, I feel unsure, and a bit tentative. I sense that Jamie is the more cautious of this pair.

Back as myself, I say, "I wonder if that is how you would *like* it to be – that you could talk about pretty much anything..." I wait a while to let those words really land, "or if that is *really* how it is?" and I look at Meg.

Meg looks back at me. I intuit (I do this by sensing into her to check it out – and also by looking at her response from the outside, which is surprisingly neutral) that Meg doesn't quite agree with Jamie, but isn't yet quite brave enough to say so. I wait a few moments. I look at Jamie, then back at Meg. Jamie is looking at Meg. Meg is looking at me. I don't say a word, but as I look at Meg I raise my eyebrows, questioning. I am inviting Meg to step forward, but I am aware that this is a delicate moment. If I push before she is ready, she will retreat. I feel as if I somehow need to align myself with her delicate (yet steely) soul, the part of her that is ready to step forward and speak her truth. I wait. I realise I am holding my breath... so I allow myself to breathe out softly, deliberately relaxing my body as I do, and it seems as if the tension in the room slightly eases too. I still don't say anything. Meg is looking at me. I smile slightly. I see her begin to realise that I know... and now she knows that I know! She recognises something in my demeanour. I see that she also knows I am waiting, allowing her to speak about it if she wants to... but I hope that she knows that I am not going to push, and she can choose not to say anything. I feel completely open-hearted and very benign, even loving, as I look at Meg. The power of this silent communication fascinates me. How much has happened in a matter of moments. Still I say nothing. Now Jamie is looking at me, questioning. Puzzled. He knows that something has happened that he is not 'in on'. He looks at Meg.

She breathes out, smiles very softly, and says guardedly, "We don't really talk openly anymore." I notice that I give an involuntary nod of support and validation. This is a really brave step, and is probably the pivotal moment that will transform their relationship. However, it isn't quite as easy as that.

"What do you mean?" asks Jamie accusingly. I jump inside his skin, and a crack has just appeared in my world. A part of me, as Jamie, is frantically trying to pull the two edges together, to hide the crack, to paper over, to turn away.

This time Meg doesn't hesitate for so long. It seems that having started, a part of her knows that she needs to lay it on the line, that there is no going back. This is her opportunity. She softly continues, "I think that we both tend to tell the other one what we think they want to hear…"

"Noooo." Jamie sounds like a man who has clung on to a ledge for many years and has finally and reluctantly had to let go. I sense inside his body… and I am blanking out. I am numb. I don't want to hear what is about to come. Gently, yet firmly now, Meg carries on: "I don't always tell you exactly how it is. I don't want to hurt you. So I think I *do* sometimes tell you what I think you want to hear rather than the whole, sometimes brutal, truth. I love you so much, I simply can't bear to hurt you."

Jamie looks puzzled. He has stopped breathing. "But I do everything for you. It's not because of me that we have problems." I feel empathy, thinking, *This is really tough for him.*

Meg looks at me, appealing. This time I step in.

"I think there is a line, a continuum: on one end is politeness, and on the other end is authenticity. I know some couples learn to stay more at the polite end, and that works for a while – but the problem over time is that they stop being honest. They can either be polite, or they can be authentic. But they haven't learnt how to be both authentic and gentle. And they haven't yet learnt that actually it can be far kinder to be authentic, even if the message is hard to hear." I pause to see how they are taking this. Meg is looking concerned and yet calm. Jamie seems to be finding this slightly easier to hear from me than from Meg – which doesn't surprise me.

I continue. "Contrary to what you would expect, for some people, it becomes harder to be honest as a couple grows closer. The more intimate they become, the less honest they are. They can tell each other everything at the start, but five years down the line, they edit everything, and many of their thoughts and opinions are not spoken."

They both look at me with surprise. I really have their attention.

"What happens is that, in the very early stages of a relationship, if you lose the other person, if they leave you, you will survive. The classic example is the man who tells his life story to a person sitting in the seat next to him on the train, and doesn't stop talking during the three-hour journey... but when he gets home cannot say more than three words to his wife." They look at one another.

"He doesn't expect to see the person on the train again, so if they disapprove of him or judge him, he doesn't have to live with that on a daily basis. And since there is only a brief connection, and he won't be seeing her again, there is no fear of losing her." I pause, letting this sink in. "Whereas, when a partner is important to you, and as the relationship progresses, it can feel more dangerous to be honest. Your partner may not like what you are going to tell them, they might condemn you, or they might leave you. So the tendency is to tell them what you think they want to hear. It feels as if being honest can put the relationship in jeopardy. So for many couples, as they become closer, it actually gets harder, not easier, to be transparently honest with one another."

Jamie nods, slowly, and I notice he is breathing now. He doesn't seem numb anymore, and is absorbing what I am saying. I appreciate his dedication and willingness to listen. I think to myself, *When he gets thrown, he seems to be able to re-gather himself quickly. That is going to really help him.*

I continue, "I remember one client, who was a lifelong Conservative voter. Six months after the start of their relationship, during an election campaign, she heard her boyfriend tell someone that he could never live with someone who was right wing, and voted for the Conservatives. They hadn't fully discussed their politics and she didn't know he felt so strongly. When they came to see me twenty-five years later, and she saw me on her own, she confided that she had always continued to vote Conservative, but never dared to tell him. For twenty-five years! She didn't want to lose him!" I paused. "So what areas might you have avoided talking about? What haven't you been fully honest about?"

Meg looks up, slightly anxiously. She takes a breath. Then launches in. "One of the things I'm going to need to talk about is the fact that I want more fun in our relationship."

Jamie nods.

"I miss spending time together simply enjoying each other's company. For example, I would like us to start hiking again, like we did in the old days."

"I'd like that too," he says. I nod, affirming him.

There is a pause... and then a little transformation takes place in front of my eyes. Meg sits up straighter, momentarily closes her eyes as if drawing on a well of courage, then turns to face Jamie, saying, "I want to work on our sex life too."

He looks startled.

Meg looks straight at him, takes a long breath in, and then slowly breathes out, smiles lovingly at him and says steadily, "I want to have more pleasure when we make love, and I think that you could get more pleasure too." Although she blushes, I notice that her voice has dropped almost half an octave, and that she has settled more deeply into her body. She seems mildly embarrassed, but her hesitancy has been replaced by the need to speak. "I don't often have an orgasm when we make love, and I know I can have them. I want us to work on making love together in a way that works better for me."

Inwardly I applaud her, and cheer. Outwardly I smile, and say, "I imagine it took a lot of courage to say that." She nods. "That's exactly the kind of thing we are talking about. Well done you." My heart is wide open to both of them. This happens to me when we hit the seam of authenticity and deep truth.

Now, when I feel into Meg, she is calm and strong. Then I feel into Jamie. As him, I feel a bit shocked, and a bit tense, but still open. I come back to my own perspective. I am surprised that Jamie was able to hear this, and has not retreated. I am glad, and think, *he really is more centred and grounded than I had initially thought. He's going to be okay.*

"This is such an important step that you two have taken. It is interesting, because I had a sense early on, Meg, that you had an inner strength that you had been hiding from Jamie, and I have watched in the last thirty minutes as you have taken a chance and shown yourself in what I imagine might be a new way?" She nods.

"And Jamie, what I love is that although I think this is news to you…" he nods, confirming my thoughts, "I see that you are very ready to hear this, and maybe a part of you even welcomes it?" He nods again. "To be honest, there was a time in this session where I thought you wouldn't be able to handle it – but you seem okay?" I smile.

He nods, "Okay-ish."

"I think this is the most important step we could have taken for this relationship. I feel very hopeful for you. Well done, both of you. Our time is up now, I will see you both next time."

Jamie and Meg: Ten Days Later

Warning to people-pleasers: your lie will comfort your partner right up until the point they discover it was a lie.

"It's been hell for me," Jamie complains. "I feel like Meg is threatening our relationship. We were doing okay I thought... and now I feel as if I am being criticised. Meg has been distant ever since our last session."

I feel into Meg, and she feels grounded, centred, concerned and loving. This makes me wonder if there is something from Jamie's history playing out here, loading this situation. Or maybe he is not used to Meg editing herself less, speaking her truth more freely, being more authentic and demonstrating a new and healthier way of being, where she has more sense of her own independence. I wait to see which of these issues (or indeed any other) emerge as most relevant.

Meg turns to Jamie. "Actually I feel very loving towards you, and I really want you to know that. I want us to work this out more than anything I have ever wanted before. But I also want us both to confront ourselves. I have been doing a lot of thinking. There were things that Juliet said in our last session that really resonated with me, that have made me realise that I need to stand up for myself now. She asked us how honest we are, and I realise I haven't been."

Jamie looks puzzled. Meg continues, "I'm sorry. In a way I have been protecting you, but also protecting myself. But you are bigger than that, and so am I. I don't need to do that. I owe it to myself to get honest, and I think I owe it to our relationship. I don't want us to split up, but if that is what has to happen, I can live with it. But I want us *both* to work on it. I think there is a deeper level of love that we can reach. And in this relationship I need to take responsibility for being me. I need to speak my truth, and I need you to hear it and respond."

Jamie looks at me, appealing for help. I could step in, rescue him, support him. Actually I think that Meg is right, and that this is a chance for them both to allow something new to happen between them. I decide to ask about her goals.

"So what needs to change, Meg? Have you been clear with Jamie about that?"

Meg turns to me and starts to tell *me*, and I gesture to Jamie, indicating that she should talk to him rather than to me.[1] This is a chance for them to practise communicating more clearly. If I am the person in the middle all the time, they will be too dependent on me to be there when they discuss difficult topics.

Meg leans forward, her voice is louder now, more forceful, demanding, "Well, I mentioned sex last time. We haven't talked about that since. Juliet was right, it is a big topic and we have to discuss that here, now."

She sounds nervous, I think. Then I say out loud, "Meg, see if you can soften your voice tone a little. It will make it easier for Jamie to hear you."

She looks taken aback, but continues more softly, looking at Jamie. "Then there is honesty. I realise I have been afraid, in many areas of my life. I tell people what I think they want to hear, and not the real truth. I've done that with you." Her gentler voice brings her vulnerability to the fore in a helpful way. "I think I have been realising that for a while, but something in our last session made me decide I don't want to live like that anymore. In fact, I don't think I can. It feels like a kind of betrayal of myself."

"It sounds like it is a matter of integrity?" I suggest.

Meg looks appreciative. "Yes. Yes, that's it."

I sense into Jamie, who is not saying much. As Jamie, I feel small, afraid, overwhelmed. I am not so grounded as last time. I feel a bit lost. *I don't know what is being demanded of me now, and I am scared. I don't know if I am up for this. I thought we were doing okay, and Meg is not behaving as I know her. She is different and I don't like it.*

I come back into my own (Juliet's) skin and say, "This must be pretty terrifying for you, Jamie? I imagine that you don't feel ready to embark on this journey, and yet it sounds like you have no choice, and that Meg has crossed some kind of a threshold and is going to go on, whether you like it or not."

Jamie looks frightened, but also relieved. It seems my guess was correct, and by naming what is happening for him, and acknowledging it, I am helping him to process some of the complex feelings he is having.

"I feel scared," he admits. "Really scared."

Meg looks at him with respect. "You don't normally own up to that kind of thing," she says gently, "and you know what, it feels good when you speak it."

I nod in agreement. I find myself marvelling at how far they have both come. Some clients are like mature fruit. You only have to place your hand under a ripe pear on a tree, and it will almost drop into your palm, whilst the under-ripe ones need to be wrenched off. Meg arrived for therapy ready to step into herself in a new way. Not only that, but she is being fairly gentle with Jamie, and yet quietly insistent. I feel very optimistic for them. *If they continue to grow in this way, they will be fine,* I think to myself.

"What is going wrong sexually?" I ask.

I see Jamie stiffen and brace himself. I imagine he is afraid of what she might say, and I feel a sudden burst of empathy for him.

"Well, nothing really," Meg says. "Except that it is okay, but not satisfying for me. It has always been alright, but I want more. I don't often orgasm during sex."

"What do you put that down to?" I ask.

"Jamie," she says.

"Gosh!" I say, thinking that this is harsh. Although if this is how she sees it, at least she is being honest. But I don't think it is the whole truth.

Here I have a choice point. I will need to take a full sexual history at some point, to see what patterns there may be. Sometimes I do that individually, so the partner doesn't have to listen as sex with previous partners is discussed. Sometimes I do it when they are together. This can be helpful when there has been emotional fusion – a pseudo closeness. It gives the couple practice at speaking, and hearing, difficult truths, which can help to make them more resilient. Telling *me* their sexual history is not as confronting as talking to each other about it. Many couples have not told each other this level of detail before, and it can be hard for their 'newer' partner to hear them talk about earlier sexual encounters. Some couples do this easily. Others have never done it. Apart from hearing their sexual history, my aim is to strengthen them, teaching them skills that will serve them well later on, when they have difficult conversations at home.

So many people think they are being generous by pleasing their partner, and believe that putting their partner's needs above their own creates the ultimate relationship. This can be genuinely helpful when done from a place of generosity and strength. But often this behaviour is driven by a combination of fear of their partner's reaction, poor boundaries and low self-esteem. This tends to perpetuate an unhealthy relationship, and is likely to lead to resentment and martyrdom. I will write more about this emotional fusion and dysfunctional togetherness in Chapter 2.

Again, I think to myself, *I don't want to be needlessly cruel, I wonder if they can handle hearing about each other's sexual history?* I am concerned about getting it wrong for them.

Then, looking at Jamie, I check. "Is it okay if I ask each of you some questions about previous partners?" He nods. I wonder to myself, *how easy would it have been for him to say 'No'?* Meg looks at him and says, "It is fine by me." I decide to give it a go, and watch their reactions carefully.

"I have been able to orgasm with one of my previous partners," she tells me, and seems quite matter of fact.

"During penetration? Or was that with manual stimulation?" I enquire.

"Both," she says with a slight smile. I think, *She is remembering something*, and I decide not to ask about it. I tune into Jamie, and he seems to be okay with this, so I continue.

"And with the others?"

"There have only been four before Jamie, and with the other three I came when they stimulated my clitoris, but not with penetration."

I decide to share some facts. "Are you aware that only 25% of women regularly have an orgasm during vaginal intercourse?"[2]

"No, I thought it was more than that," Meg responds. "Well, that is interesting, because it only happened a handful of times even with the best one." I feel into her, she is sobered, considering. I sense into Jamie, he is doing alright, in fact he seems relieved.

I pause for a while, and then looking at Jamie I ask, "How adventurous are you sexually?"

"Not very, I would say." He glances at Meg who nods. "I think I am fairly traditional. I haven't got exploratory with positions and things. I tend to stick to what I like." He has surprised me again. I respect his honesty about this, as I can see it is not easy for him.

31

Meg sounds cross. "And that is the problem. It is a bit samey. Following a formula, and I don't like it." I notice that just as Jamie opens up, Meg criticises him. I hope it doesn't stop him being honest. I see this so often. Meg is asking Jamie to come forward, but when he does, she finds it hard to handle, and criticises him, which is likely to shut him down again. I won't comment on it until she has done it a few times, but I note it.

"So part of what you want is some more variety?" I ask.

"Yes," she responds.

I go on. "Sex is really interesting. When we are nine or ten-years-old we think kissing with tongues is disgusting. By the time we are in our teens most of us enjoy that, but we might think oral sex is disgusting. The way sex often seems to work is that when two people meet, one of them communicates, 'Well I think a, b, c and d is disgusting and perverted and I don't want to do that.' The other then conveys, 'Well I think x and y is perverted and I never want to do that!' And they end up doing whatever is left. So sex consists of leftovers!"[3]

"Yep. That is us," Meg says. "Only, I wasn't entirely honest, right from the beginning. I held back. I didn't want to seem like I was a slut, and so I didn't let Jamie know that I love oral sex, and that I like to be adventurous."

"You were protecting him, not wanting to hurt his feelings?" I ask.

Jamie says defensively, "I would have been up for more adventure."

There is a part of me that doubts that this was true when they met a few years ago, but I hope that it might be true now. He is going to have to learn about tolerating discomfort[4] in order to let himself grow. There will be embarrassing moments and difficult feelings that he will have to stay with. He is going to have to push through his reserve. He will probably have to try out behaviours that he might have thought were disgusting, and he will find that challenging. I look at him, and I am surprised how hopeful I feel for them. *Yes, I think you'll really be up for this.*

We continue our conversation, touching on many things: trying out different positions, mild bondage, anal sex, using pornography, reading erotic literature, using sex toys, verbalising sexual fantasies, and using role play during sex.

"That is a step too far for me right now. I can't imagine coming in as Antony to your Cleopatra! Or swinging from the chandeliers." Jamie laughs. I note his laugh, it is genuine. He has stepped into the more relaxed place again, and I see that as a good sign. He quickly swings from feeling threatened to feeling okay, and back again.

I come in. "No, but maybe you could be yourselves, and pretend you have never met. You meet up in a bar, and chat her up as if she was a stranger, and see where that goes?" I want to let him see that there are many different kinds of role play that they could experiment with.

Then I come back to Meg's orgasm. "How easy is it for you to orgasm during masturbation?" I check.

"I'm not sure. Sometimes I can come really quickly, but usually it takes me a good twenty to thirty minutes on my own."

"And with Jamie masturbating you?" I ask.

"We haven't tried that much," she says, and it turns out that they only did it once.

"It took about three-quarters of an hour," Jamie said, shamefacedly. "I wasn't very good at it."

"Is that why you haven't tried it again?" I ask.

"Maybe," he says.

"Did you know that the average woman, from a 'cold start' to full orgasm, takes anything between twenty and forty minutes? So that was perfectly normal," I say.

Jamie looks amazed. Even Meg looks surprised.

"I thought it was me," says Jamie. "I thought I wasn't doing it right, and I guess I felt embarrassed and I didn't want to talk about it, so I just stopped, and didn't try."

"And I thought there was something wrong with me, taking so long, so I haven't wanted to raise it, though I think about it almost every time we make love."

"But you never mentioned it." Jamie reddens.

"Nor did you," says Meg gently, and Jamie nods.

The session continues. Meg is gently pushing, standing up for herself. I respect her more and more, and I suspect Jamie does too, though he doesn't acknowledge that. But he follows her lead, and seems to become more and more open as the session goes on, and that touches me too. They have agreed to try out a variety of new things before our next session. I wonder how their sex life will be next time we meet, and what their journey is going to entail. I reflect on how much I enjoy my job, and what a privilege it is to have such an insight into the intimate details of peoples' lives.

Time passes, and it is our penultimate session. Towards the end of it, I acknowledge some of their journey: "Meg, I love the changes that you have made. I respect the push for honesty that you have brought to the relationship, and the courage you have shown, speaking truths that you found difficult to voice. And Jamie," I turn to look at him now, "you have changed *so* much. When I think of how you were when you first came, quite straight-laced really – and now look at you! You are quite often the one moving the sexual side of things along. It is a big change." Meg nods cautiously. "I know Meg wants more, but I think it is important to acknowledge how far you have come." Meg smiles and nods, and I know she can agree with this. They look lovingly at one another. As they leave, they each give me a heartfelt hug. I feel very moved.

Thoughts and Theory:
Gaining Different Perspectives

It is a narrow mind which cannot look at a subject
from various points of view.
George Eliot[5]

As a child, living with a father who could sulk for England, I learned how to step inside the skin of someone else to work out what is going on. When, as part of my training to be a therapist, I studied Neuro-linguistic Programming (NLP) I was surprised to discover this is an explicit and learnable skill. It forms part of the model known as Perceptual Positions, or First Second and Third Positions, or Perspectives. From an NLP point of view, I had been a natural practitioner of Second Position.

The three perspectives

To be in First Position is to be yourself, standing firmly in your own perspective, with your own values, beliefs and assumptions. A strong First Position means that you have clarity about what you think, feel and want. Being in Second Position means you have stepped into someone else's viewpoint: 'To know another person you have to walk a mile in their shoes.' You see the world from their perspective, with *their* values, beliefs and assumptions. It is as if you are experiencing the world through their eyes, and ears, and feeling what they are feeling. A good

Second Position is the basis for compassion and empathy. To stand in Third Position is to be in an impartial observer position, without the feelings of First Position or of Second Position. For Third Position, I think of someone standing on a balcony, looking down, seeing an argument in the street, and watching the two people and the disagreement, as it unfolds, watching the scene in a completely dispassionate way. But then imagine that one of the people in the argument is *you*! When you are in Third Position you still see it as if from above, from outside yourself, remaining completely detached.

As I grew up, I became more and more able to slip into Second Position, and, to some extent, into Third Position. Ironically (and this surprises many people, who don't really see how this is possible), the weakest one for me was First Position! I didn't really know what I wanted. Funnily enough, I knew what I *didn't* want, but not what I *wanted*. I remember my first husband asking me, "Where would you like to go out to eat?"

My reply was "I don't mind", which I thought at the time was true. What would have been more accurate is, *I cannot access that information right now.*

So he would suggest, "How about an Indian?"

"No, I don't want an Indian tonight," I would reply.

"How about a Chinese?"

"No, I don't want a Chinese," I would reply

"What *do* you want?" he would say, in exasperation.

"I don't know!" I would wail.

By this stage we would both be frustrated. Finally, he would luck upon the one I wanted.

"How about the Italian trattoria?"

"Perfect," I would respond, with huge relief and some gratitude.

Learning to *know* what I wanted (my First Position), and to be able to ask for it, probably took me eight years! Now I do know (and I give you a few tips for developing First Position later on in this section).

We all have our favourite: but this gives a narrow view

Once we become aware that these different perspectives are possible, we can work out which is the one we find easiest and like most, which is our second favourite and which is the one we use the least. It is wise to practise your least favourite, becoming so flexible that you can access any of the three positions in the blink of an eye, even in a challenging situation. There is a lot of useful information in each of them and, in order to get a complete picture, we need to be able to step in and out of them all. Having just one perspective alone gives you a very narrow view. Wisdom unfolds, and solutions to problems arise, when we are able to dance with, and between, all three perspectives.

As a therapist, my clients benefit from my ability to Second Position them, to step inside their skin and get a sense of what might be going on for them. I develop compassion, empathy and am able to gain access to otherwise inaccessible information. Having now developed a good-enough First position (my husband might say my First Position has become too good!), I don't become over entangled with my clients' world views and lose my own (which used to happen). My First Position has helped me to say, 'No' to work and to new clients when my schedule is too busy and I really cannot fit it in. Twelve years ago, when my First Position was poor, I would say, 'Yes' to new clients even when I didn't have space, and then regret it later. I was prioritising my clients' needs above my own. Shifting into Third Position helps me to step back, and take a dispassionate perspective of my clients, an overview of their relationship, and how the work with me is progressing (or not!).

How to do Second Position

Recently people have asked me, "How do you do that Second Position thing? How *do* you step into someone else's experience?" The answer is that I don't really know, but I do know that it is a core aspect of the way that I work. It is as if I put myself into my client's world, completely taking on their beliefs, their world view, their values, and even imagining what it would be like if I had their body shape and muscular structure. You will see me doing this with the clients throughout this book.

I don't spend very long in their world at any one time. I usually 'dip in' for a matter of moments, sometimes seconds and at the most a few minutes. It is almost as if I put myself into their body, or maybe it is more accurate to say I am putting myself into their world. In reality, of course, I am still in my own self, but I seem to be able to access information through this practice that I can't in any other way. I have been doing it so long that it seems I can often sense what they are feeling, hearing and seeing. I never assume I am correct. Rather, I use this technique as a map, to tentatively guide me through the territory of the client's world, and then, crucially, I check out what I have sensed with them. When I get it right, it can be really useful. Sometimes I can feel and discover information that the other person has not yet recognised. I can't do it all the time. There are occasions where I simply cannot attune to the person in front of me. This maybe because the gulf between us is too large, but is more likely to be because I am tense, angry, or trying too hard!

In a therapy session I use Second Position to help couples understand one another. For example, I step right inside Jamie's world, and then tell Meg, "I think what might be happening is that Jamie…" and I offer her my sense of how Jamie feels about what she has said, or about the problem they are discussing. This works because couples get into habits with each other, and expect the customary response from their partner. I come in with a pair of fresh eyes, and may see things differently. I don't have their history or their baggage, and I am willing to name it as I see it. Sometimes I am wrong, and sometimes right. I learn if I'm on the right track or not by checking, in my peripheral vision, to see if Jamie is nodding or not.

So how did I learn it? As I mentioned at the beginning of the chapter, the first time I practised Second Position consciously was when I was studying NLP.[6] During the course, we were asked to pair up with another participant – we had to pick someone who we felt was very different to us. I chose Jeff. He was over six foot tall, fit, optimistic and curious. I am plump, five foot four, and in those days I lived in a world that was largely grey. I wasn't depressed as such, but certainly I had a melancholic air around me. We received our instructions. He was told to go for a walk, in his usual style, paying no attention to me. I was to follow him, not speaking or making contact, and gradually and increasingly mirror, or mimic him, until I felt I was walking in exactly the way he was (or at least as close as possible, given my legs were probably nine inches shorter than his!) I was to follow him for forty minutes, then we would change over. Julian Russell, the trainer delivering the workshop, asked each 'follower' to step into a 'modelling state', which meant changing the focus of my eyes to a soft gaze with a wide peripheral field of vision, quietening my internal dialogue and inner chatter, and carrying as little tension in my body as possible. Then Jeff began walking. He headed out of the hotel, crossed the road, and went into Kensington Gardens. Following two paces behind him, I watched, and gradually started to imitate. I followed his cadence, speed, the fluidity of his body, how upright he was, the angle of his hips, the way in which he placed each foot. His arms were free, moving easily. His head was up, held high. I was surprised to discover the pleasure I felt allowing my hips to sway! My body felt lithe – a new experience! For almost ten minutes I focussed on imitating the general shape of him as he walked. And then I moved onto the next stage: noticing and copying where his eyes were looking. That was when the truly extraordinary shift happened. My world changed.

I had never realised, until that moment, that I had always kept my body rather still as I walked, with my shoulders slightly hunched forward, looking down at the ground. Jeff was freer and had more movement in his body. He also had a completely different perspective. Sometimes he watched something straight ahead, but more often he looked up into the trees, at birds, at kites, and at the sky! As I walked, with my head held unusually high for me, my eyes began to see things I would never normally have noticed. What's more, I discovered that my hearing changed. I started tuning into sounds that I didn't normally detect: children laughing and playing Frisbee in the far distance, a dog barking, a blackbird singing, the sound of the wind in the trees and the rattle of a pram being pushed along. Unknowingly, I had always walked in a slightly self-protective manner, hunching over and shutting my world down. This man, who walked ahead of me, had his chest open and full, and his shoulders back. As I mirrored him I felt my breathing settle lower into my body, and my heart begin to open. I felt more available and connected to the world. As he gradually made his way back to the Columbia Hotel to rejoin the workshop, with me still following and mirroring, I noticed features on the buildings that I had never spotted before, such as a pile of pigeon droppings on a window ledge that must have taken years to create. It all had a strange, quirky kind of beauty. A whole world that I had missed until now had newly opened up to me. I had discovered it simply by deliberately mirroring Jeff's physiology, and the quality and direction of his attention.

After that, in the workshop, we did a number of exercises designed to help us step into experiences that were outside our habitual world. I remember a friend, who was fluent in three languages, telling me that she thinks and feels very differently when speaking German, or talking in Italian. In the exercises, I learnt that simply by using different English language patterns I could feel differently. If I talked about what 'I *need* to do', '*have* to do', and '*should* do', I recognised that I had different feelings and sensations in my body than if I said 'I *choose* to do this' and 'I *want* to do that'. Changing my voice tone, volume and speed and noticing (and changing) where in my head or body I located my voice (whether I spoke half an octave higher or lower) also had an impact on me. I learnt that I could bring about changes in myself by altering my physiology, my language, or my breathing, or by practising the different positions, of First, Second and Third. This has helped me to shift some fixed and unhelpful patterns and ways of seeing the world.

The importance of beliefs

Then came beliefs. In the workshop I was invited to connect with a belief that 'the world is a dangerous place', and to walk around the room and observe what I noticed. I saw sharp corners on tables, people who were a threat to me, and objects on the floor that I could fall over. Then I was asked to close my eyes, shake off that belief, and take on the new belief that 'the world is a completely safe place'. Opening my eyes to another perspective, I walked around the same room, with the same people, and realised I was noticing completely different things. This time people looked friendly, I noticed smiles. I saw the sun streaming through the window, a vase of red and white Sweet Williams, and the bottles of water that were provided for participants. I was struck by the instantaneous difference a change in beliefs made.

During the week-long workshop, I had many opportunities to practise opening up to see the world differently, to let go of my habitual view and expectations of people and the world around me. I began to learn how to maintain a state of openness and curiosity.

Later, when I started to learn about neuroscience, I found out about mirror neurones. We all have these, though research indicates that there is less mirror neurone activity in those with autism than with neuro-typical people. So, talking for a moment about those people we call 'normal', when we watch something happen to someone else, the mirror neurones in our own brain fire. For example, imagine watching someone pricking themselves with a needle. You may wince at the thought of that, as if you can feel it too.

So, in answer to the question, *How did you learn to do Second Position?* I think I was lucky to have the latent skills I'd learned as a child, which were then fostered through my NLP training. By developing my flexibility, by practising different physiological and psychological states, I improved my ability to tune in to my own body, recognise subtle changes in my thinking and emotions, and work out how to 'read' these. At the same time I learnt how to quieten my internal noise, so that I do not have 'thinking and chatter' going on inside *my* head to distract me. I use a soft peripheral focus, suspending my own perspective, expectations, agenda and judgements, and consciously ease out any excess tensions in my body. If any of *my* 'baggage' comes in (for example, anxiety or anger), then I gently acknowledge it, thank it, and move it to one side. I want, when with clients, to sit in an open state of gentle curiosity, willing to enjoy a completely new and unexpected experience.

Finally, during a therapy session, I imagine making the same face or gesture the client is making (probably by using my mirror neurones) and notice what impact that has on me, how does it make *me* feel. Over the years I have learnt to discriminate between thoughts, feelings and emotions that are mine, and those that have come in from someone else. Basically I think that I have learnt to stimulate (and simulate) neurological patterns that are not *my* normal ones, and then I can come back and report on the data I have found from doing that. All of this has developed my 'intuition', so that I can 'guess' what someone may be feeling and get it right, much of the time.

If you are intrigued about this and decide to explore the skill of Second Position, here are some pointers. Firstly, try and find some people who are really different, from you and from each other. For example, practise with a seven-year-old child, a ninety-year-old woman, and a twenty-year-old rugby player. And I have a tip for you. Attempt it with people who are not close to you to start with. It is much harder to go into Second Position when you have an opposing point of view, a strong agenda, or feel cross with them! Start with people who you feel friendly towards, or at the very least, neutral. When you feel like stretching yourself, find a work of art that touches your soul, and take Second Position with that, be it a painting, a sculpture or a piece of music. *Be* the painting, *feel inside* the sculpture, or experience the music *as if you yourself are the instruments* being played! It can be informative and interesting as well as a lot of fun.

Developing First Position

If you want or need to develop your First Position, here are a few tips. Since my First Position started out so weak, it took seven to eight years before I developed a strong one.

To begin with, check that you are looking through your own eyes and hearing through your own ears ('associated'), rather than looking at yourself-from-outside (which is 'disassociated'). I started by using the words 'I' and '*myself*' and '*me*' more often. I decided to practise tuning in to myself moment by moment. I used to ask myself, *What do I want right now?* The answer might be *a deep breath.* I would take a deep breath. Then, only 2 minutes later, I would ask myself, *What do I want right now?* Giving myself a moment to hear the whisper of a response, I realise it is *a sip of water.* I have a drink. Then, a few minutes later: *And now, now what do I want?* The answer...*to stretch and move my shoulders.* Once I knew, I always tried to respond, to reward my body for letting me know. Little by little I learnt how to tune in to what my body wanted, and then to listen to the more subtle murmurs that came from my soul. Over time the answers came more quickly and clearly, and then unbidden. The communication path had become clearer, and I had re-developed the compass of my first position. Sometimes there were conflicting wants, such as to go to bed but not to miss the end of the film. And there were times when my wants clashed with someone else's. But at least I was now in a position to choose.

Developing Third Position

Developing Third Position was not such a challenge for me. In Third Position you have information from First and from Second Position, but you are not caught in the feelings of either. You are outside the communication loop. Think of having the perspective of a cameraman who is filming an event, or a helicopter view looking down from above. You are standing back, out of the action, breathing evenly and easily. If you are sitting, then it helps to lean back. As you think about, or talk about the people involved (including yourself), refer to everyone in the third person. For example: "Oh look. Kate has just hit Juliet," (as opposed to "Oh look, Kate has just hit *me*.") Be curious about what is happening and how it is unfolding. Allow your anger and judgement to be temporarily suspended. It is important to practise Third Position when you are *not* emotionally involved in situations, so that you develop the skills of being able to step out. Then, when you are in the middle of a powerful emotional event, you will find that you can draw on these resources, because you have already learned how to use the tools. Remember too, that Third Position is a really helpful stress management tool, and very useful when you want to self-soothe (more about that in Chapter 3).

Practise all three perspectives

I teach this tool explicitly to many of my clients. Developing all three perspectives helps couples to disentangle when things start to become over-emotional, by moving from First to Third Position, allowing them to access their thinking and resources, even in stressful situations. It is also really valuable for the people who get overly invested in their partner (too much Second Position). They often need to learn how to step more into their own perspective (First Position) – Meg, who featured earlier, was intuitively starting to do this. My intention with Jamie was to help him develop a healthy Second Position (to help him be more curious about what Meg wanted), combined with a more positive First Position (so he would be willing to step forward to stay engaged with her, rather than pulling back due to his lack of confidence). For those who find intimacy too much, and who might disconnect as a way of coping (over-using Third Position), stepping into Second Position helps them to be more understanding and considerate with their partner.

Chapter 2

Frank and Maxine

Love is an irresistible desire to be irresistibly desired.
Robert Frost[1]

They sit in my therapy room. Frank looks defeated. Maxine is furious. Furious! "If it wasn't for him, his lack of caring, his indifference, not to mention the fact that he flirts with other women… I know I can't trust him," she whines. "If only he would pay *me* attention…" She doesn't bother to finish the sentence, but I imagine she'd say *if only he would pay me attention then everything would be okay.*

I put myself in his shoes. How would I feel living with this fireball of fury? Every fibre of her fulminating against who I am. With each breath she condemns me, hates me, shrinks me. I am helpless in front of this onslaught. This vitriol. *Why on earth is she still with me?*

Then he speaks. Slow, steady, bringing order and calm – or trying to. Changing the energy. "It's impossible to talk to her when she's like this." He glances at her, his look loaded with a decade of judgement. "Too much emotion. We can't connect when she's emotional." And here they show me their stuckness.

I have several different reactions all at the same time. The first is helplessness. How on earth can we get out of this painful place?

I feel the weight of grief underneath his cloak of calm. Her pain carries a gut-wrenching agony that penetrates me. The second reaction is compassion. How can they live with this? The third is a kind of rightness. *This is real, this is truth. We are right here, where the work is needed. But what to say? My next words will be important, I have to get it right (or right enough). Or rather I have to be careful, watching as I speak, reading their reactions to what I am saying. Too strong, and they may not be able to bear the pain, too sugary sweet or too hopeful and they won't trust me.* I pause, giving myself time. I know how important it is that I stay real. That is what I have to offer, my honesty. But I also hold the place of hope.

"This is really painful," I say. They both nod. I notice this moment of agreement between them. "I imagine this has been going on for a while?" Again, both nod. "And you could separate, but I imagine a part of you hopes that you won't, or you wouldn't be here." I state this, rather than asking the question, but I notice they don't nod this time. In reaction to the absence of a nod, I say, "Or maybe you feel like this is the end of the road, and separation is the only option?" I notice that Maxine almost imperceptibly nods, and breathes out, and I realise she has been holding her breath for a long time. Something in the room eases, a very slight shift in the energy, a small relief. I wonder if it is because I have brought in the idea of separation. It has been named.

This prompts me to talk about the way I work. "Usually I help couples to stay together. That is the focus of my work, until one or both of you tell me that you want to separate, and then my job is to help you do that with dignity. However, in that process, we might well explore what it would mean to each of you to separate, and how that could work, to see if it might be a realistic option. But my main focus is to work with you two to stay together. Does that sound okay?" Again they nod.

"And you will never get back the relationship you started with," I say. "That is over. Finished. Gone. The task now is to help you find a relationship that is good enough, that you both want to buy into. To help you work out what would make you really *want* to stay together. So one of the things we need to do is to get clear about that. Does that sound helpful?" They cautiously nod. "What do you hope to get from coming here?"

Frank starts speaking. His presence and voice fill the room. I wonder if he is really as calm on the inside as he appears on the outside. I suspect not. Despite his obvious attempts to present himself well – the smart suit, impeccably polished shoes, crisp Jermyn Street shirt and gold cufflinks – he also has a wearied and fragile quality. There is something in the way he talks that I can't quite name. It is as if he is appealing to me to see past the disguise, to read his despair. As I begin to feel into where he is coming from, I sense that he is at the end of his tether.

"I love Maxine. I always have. I just want to make it right between us. Nothing I do seems to help. I've tried everything, and it isn't enough. Maybe the kindest thing is for me to go. I sure as hell don't make her happy. So I guess I want to know what I should do." Now a tiny quake enters his voice. "What can I do that will help… should I leave? I think that is what she wants."

As I tune into my body, my heart begins to open, responding to his vulnerability, and hearing how defeated he feels.

Now it is her turn. "I wish I could feel his love. He says it occasionally, but I don't feel it. I don't know what the block is, but I don't believe him. I guess he is not affectionate with me, and if he does give me a hug I know it is because he wants sex. So then I pull back. I don't want to be a sex object." She sounds defeated too.

Again I feel the stuckness. It is a hollow place, with no signposts. A well of grief, distress, hurt, anger, and fury. Underneath, it is as if they are saying, *we have tried everything, we can't be bothered anymore. It is all too much pain and effort.*

But isn't this just the normal stuff of relationships? Yes, they have gone a bit further down the road of despair than I might have done – but they are still together. Just. We seem to have a myth that relationships are easy, it is the 'happy ever after' scenario that occurs when the prince meets the princess. Once you have done the difficult thing of meeting the 'right one', then the rest just happens. Relationships should be effortless!

Something sometimes arises as I sit with clients who are in therapy. It is what the psychologist James Hillman would call an imaginal process[2] not only being with 'what is' (using Second Position), but taking it a step further, to imagine what 'might be'. Attuning myself to the tiny, unspoken messages and signals in the room, I hypothesise that if I had a session with Maxine on her own she may say, *I hate him. And I hate myself. I want to give up.* I might sit there, not saying much. Not trying to change her mind, or make it easier. Simply breathing and staying with her. But after a few moments she might go on, now sounding defeated. *But if I give up I will be a failure.* Feeling her pain, I continue my reverie. She'd say, *Being single will show I am useless. Single. Again.* Contempt for herself would drench the room. This is a lot to surmise from so little time with them, but there is something unspoken, hanging in the air between us, that takes me right to this point.

Then I empathically envisage a one-to-one session with Frank. I imagine him saying, *It's her fault. Not mine. I have really tried. And she has let me down.* I sit, breathing, offering myself as a witness, and in my mind's eye I see him continuing. *I have invested too much to let this go... It's going to cost me a lot of money if we split.* I wait. Minutes pass. Then, I picture him starting to cry, *I can't bear to live without her.* Sobbing now, he says, *I've never actually lived on my own and I'm scared!* Silence as he absorbs this shocking revelation. *And I don't want to be the one that gives up. She's going to have to make the decision...* Another minute passes, and I imagine him quietly admitting, *I'm terrified. I'm terrified that I will never find anyone else.*

I think these may be the double binds that they are fighting. If I am right, then whatever decision they make, they will feel like they can't win. The essence of her struggle is this: *I hate him and I want to leave. But if I give up I will have failed, and I can't bear to fail again.* His double bind is: *It's her fault. Why should I have to pick up the cost of that? I will stay to spite her...* but underneath that, driving him, is: *actually I'm terrified of leaving.* There is no good solution to this; at least if you stay in their perspectives, there is no easy way out.

These impressions of Frank and Maxine have been so strong that I am curious to see if I am on track, or way off! I let them flood into me, informing me. But, never sure that I am right, and knowing there's a greater complexity than I've so far seen, I keep an open mind and a willingness to be wrong. I am on the lookout for instances that don't fit my hypothesis, as well as examples that do.

I like Harville Hendrix's idea[3] of the three stages of a relationship: the 'ideal', the 'ordeal' and the 'real deal'. There is the romantic phase, where we can't get enough of each other, the sex is fantastic, and we hang on our partner's every word. Then the ordeal: the power struggle, the part where it gets difficult. We realise our partner is not perfect, and maybe they don't adore us in the way that they should. Other things take them away from us, such as their work, hobbies, or friends. Alternatively, they are too demanding and clingy, not wanting us to take any space. It is sad to note that when many couples hit the ordeal phase, we think that this is the relationship going wrong, and give up. But if we get through this stage, then we often find the 'real deal'. A deep, abiding love, a companionship, a place of trust and respect. Generally, this more harmonious phase will last for a while, until something happens that pushes us back in to the 'ordeal' again, when we face another choice point. Stay together, or split up. If we stay together, if we *choose* to stay together, then we may touch the 'ideal' again for a while. Sex may be re-invigorated, and certainly we will bask in their love for a while, before we settle in to the 'real deal' again. We cycle round and round these three phases.

I explain the 'ideal, ordeal and real deal' to Frank and Maxine briefly, and then continue. "There is a therapist called David Schnarch[4] who says, 'Emotionally committed relationships are people-growing-machines.' That is what is happening here. The relationship that you used to have does not work anymore. In order to engage in the next stage of relationship you are both going to need to grow, and this can feel painful. But you are in the right place to think about that. It is my job to help you shift and grow, and look at this differently, so you can decide if you want to continue the relationship – or if the better choice for you is to split up. But, as a couples therapist, one of the things that I commonly see is that when a couple splits up, they find a new partner and get into an extraordinarily similar dynamic. Then, a few years later, when they hit the 'ordeal' phase again, the power-struggle stage, they leave that relationship too. So you could save yourself five years and just work on this relationship now!"

They live three hours' drive away from me, too far to attend for weekly sessions. So they have come for an intensive 'couples in calamity' session, which is seven hours of therapy, spread over two days. We will be together for three and a half hours today, and the same again tomorrow. This means I have some time to really help them see things differently; it is concentrated but not rushed. I suggest that they take it in turns to go for a half-hour walk. This gives them a break, and allows me to have some one-to-one time with each of them. Maxine leaves first. I think she is relieved to get out of the pressure of my little room, and take some space. I ask Frank what is really going on for him. He talks to me more freely, now he doesn't have to 'edit' what he is saying, or carefully phrase it so that it doesn't hurt Maxine. We can cut to the core of what is going on, and don't need to pussyfoot around.

I check how serious he is about leaving. It becomes clear that despite being at his wits' end, he is still very devoted to Maxine, but he finds it hard to show this. He would love to find a way to pull this relationship back from the brink. He considers leaving – and tells me again that his leaving would be an act of love, since she is so unhappy with him. Although I suspect (and voice the thought) that this would be a repeat of his pattern of withdrawing when the going gets tough.

"Yes," he admits. He pauses to reflect, then continues, "I do retreat, into my shell." He continues, "If she wants to talk she won't let up, she just comes after me again and again. Sometimes, I take the dog for a walk just to get away from her. So yes, I have learnt to hide."

I gently say, "When you talk about leaving, you may think you would be leaving for her, but I think that you would be exiting because you can't handle the strength of your *own* feelings. Really you would be doing it for yourself, not for her."

When I see Maxine on her own I am struck by how unloved she feels, and how uncertain of Frank's love. Many things contribute to this, not least of which is Maxine's history with her own father, who had very little time when she was a child. He openly preferred her older blonde sister, his first born, who found school easy and was top of her class. He didn't seem to like Maxine.

Having told me about her father, she then goes on to give me lots of examples of Frank's lack of love for her. She tells me that although she quite enjoys sex, what is much more important to her is to be wanted by Frank. She withholds sexually, because she doesn't feel wanted, so they only make love occasionally.

"Sex is usually okay when we are on holiday. But at home, well. You'll say it is my fault."

I am piqued, and curious to see what she thinks I would blame her for.

She continues, "I push him away if he makes an approach, and I go up to bed before him, so I am asleep when he comes up. But I am not ready to talk about this today. I've tried and tried talking things through, and that doesn't work. He won't. I know that if we go to bed at the same time then all he wants is a sexual release, and I just don't want that. He doesn't desire *me*. It happens in so many areas of our relationship: he does what *he* wants. He prioritises himself."

I realise that there are big relationship issues that need dealing with first, before we can tackle the sexual problems. Maxine and Frank's dynamic consists of several parts. The first problem is her difficulty believing anything positive that he says to her, or about her. I suspect this blueprint comes from her childhood. I have already noticed that whenever Frank looks at her with love or makes a loving comment, she completely disregards it, not seeming to notice. Secondly, she ties her sense of self-esteem to Frank's approval of her. She tells me that she is desperate for his reassurance, but shows me that she cannot take it in. Thirdly, she uses his behaviour towards other women to evaluate her own importance. If he flirts, she feels rejected and insignificant. She doesn't realise that his old habits of withdrawing from her and flirting with others are probably due to *his* childhood, and nothing to do with her. She fears that the relationship won't last, despite the fact that they have been together for twenty-five years.

I make a choice, and I let her know that he has shared with me how deeply he loves her. She looks shocked. I repeat it. "He loves you. You may not see it, or he may not show you how much he loves you in ways that are obvious to you, but I have no doubt that he does." I could see that this was a pivotal moment for Maxine. In the two hours we had spent together she had decided she could trust me. I didn't bullshit her. Earlier, I had not sugar-coated the situation, and this was paying off now. Again I repeat it, looking her right in the eyes, and delivering my message while opening myself so that I am completely transparent and connected throughout my body (which brings tears to my eyes). I say, "I utterly believe that he really loves you." Despite most of her believing Frank doesn't care, a part of her begins to listen to me. I say it again, looking not only at her, but deep inside her, which is where I am hoping this message will land. "He really does love you, and I think it would be really helpful if you could let yourself feel that. I saw it myself earlier. He looked at you with such love. But it's as if you miss a lot of those signs."

Watching Maxine carefully, I see her purse her lips as she moves from scornful, to sceptical. Then her face softens and I see the yearning, longing-to-believe-that-it-could-be-true. Suddenly she turns her attention to me, evaluating me again, checking if this is *really* true. I focus on my breath for a moment, breathing out gently so that my body is relaxed and absolutely open to her scrutiny. She sees that *I* really believe that he loves her. Then I spot the shift beginning: as she opens to the possibility that maybe-he-does-love-her. A moment passes. She's looking down, but in that unseeing way that people have when they are remembering something. I wonder if she is thinking back over their recent past together? I hope that she is looking for signs that he does love her, signs that she may have missed before. As her face reddens and tears spill onto her cheeks, she looks at me. I see the dawning realisation, as some part of her begins to accept, on the deepest level, that he does love her, and she smiles, relieved. All this occurs in slightly less than ten minutes.

When Frank walks in through the door, he looks directly at Maxine, and she gives him a shy smile. Things feel different. He glances at me, curious. I look at Maxine. She says to Frank, "I think there are some things I have been missing. Maybe I have been looking at things through a very dark lens and seeing problems." Frank gives a huge sigh, relaxes a little, and smiles. "I have been thinking too," he says. "We have too much together to throw this away. In the past we were a really good team. I want that for us again now." And so it goes on for some minutes, as the two of them slowly inch back towards each other. I put this down to two key things. One is the shift that she has just made, to believing that he loves her, which opens her to him. The other is his recognition that his leaving would be for him and not for her.

On the second day we explore childhood patterns that have contributed to their problems. Maxine recognises she had never felt good enough for her father. Frank realises he has copied his father's pattern of withdrawing whenever there was trouble. "I get overwhelmed by too much attention," he says. "Both my parents tended to be indifferent to me and I am not used to attention – I have learnt to look after myself. I had to do that as a child, because no one else was looking out for me. And although I want Maxine's love and attention, I reject it." I smile. This feels like a big acknowledgement.

Both of them are feeling really good about their progress, but I come in. "There is still a lot of work to do. Let's not pretend that it is all okay now. We have just taken the first step, and there is a long way to go. My thinking is that you should let this session settle and do its work, and see how you are after this. There will be habits to break, and new routines to create. As you communicate in new ways, you will notice that you are changing your unhelpful patterns, such as automatically blaming the other. As you both said, today it felt too soon to talk about sex, because there has been too much pain and hurt from the relationship. But it is a long time since you had sex. Of course. Why would you want to make love when you are so angry with one another? But as the work on the relationship settles in, and the work we have done today makes an impact on you both, things will change. You will discover you can *trust* the changes, and then, when you feel ready for the next step, we should meet again and work out how to help you move back to a regular love life in the fullest sense of the word." Frank looks really pleased at that! For him, the fact that Maxine doesn't want to make love is a sign that she doesn't care about him. If we could re-invigorate their sex life, then that would help him be able to be more loving. There is an old cliché that 'women need to feel loved in order to want sex, and men need to have sex in order to feel loving'. I feel that this is true for Maxine and Frank.

We talk about what they will do in the future. I advise Maxine to take a break when she feels herself getting wound up. Because she has an ability to twist and twist herself into a ball of wrath, it is important for her, if they have a row and she gets wound up, to take some time out. She needs to take twenty to thirty minutes to let herself cool down and compose herself before they continue. Maxine has no trouble connecting to her emotions – for her the challenge is to keep her 'thinking self' available. Frank, on the other hand, needs to move from his thinking to his feelings, and his job is to stay with his emotions and to connect with the sensations in his body, to see if he can discover exactly what he is feeling.

We also talk about activities they could do together: easy, fun things. They agree to go for a two-hour walk. Maxine would work out a route, and Frank (who never normally had anything to do with supermarket shopping or cooking) would buy a picnic to take with them. Then they agree to take it in turns to come up with a plan for some pleasurable joint activity. They set out to do a fun thing together at least once a fortnight.

I reflect on how different the energy in the room feels now. The hope has come back. I ask them to imagine that they have planted some delicate new saplings, which will thrive given the right conditions. However, if a herd of goats happens to come by, they won't stand a chance. The goats will eat them up in seconds.

In this session we have planted saplings, but we need to put a protective cage around each one, so they won't get damaged. I ask them to be gentle with one another, and help each other notice when the habitual, unhelpful behaviours begin. They decide to use a code word 'sausages' when either one of them feels the other reverting to old patterns. It makes them laugh when they say it, and I hope it will make them laugh when things are tense at home.

The room I use for therapy is at the end of my garden, and William, my husband, was at home writing on the top floor of the house which is 150 yards away. When I saw him that evening, he said, "You did a good job with the couple who came at ten o'clock. They arrived looking really distant – but they left holding hands!"

Frank and Maxine: Six Months Later

Don't put the key to your happiness in someone else's pocket.
Unknown

F rank and Maxine have made good progress. We have met three times: the first 'couples in calamity' session and then twice more, each time for a three-hour session. Supporting Maxine to develop her confidence and sense of self has been a vital part of the therapy. This has helped her stand on her own two feet, as a separate individual, not so dependent on Frank. This is part of her journey to find her own authority, a process called 'differentiation'. Differentiation is our ability to be able to balance the urge to be emotionally connected with our desire to be free, autonomous, and direct our own life.

'Emotional fusion' is the opposite of differentiation. When a couple are fused, as Frank and Maxine were when they first arrived, they easily lose their emotional balance within the relationship. Maxine loses her balance when left 'on her own' and is dependent on Frank to keep herself feeling okay. Frank gets overwhelmed by too much closeness, and so has to take space to regain his balance. Just as part of the work had been to help Maxine strengthen herself so that she was no longer dependent on Frank's view of her to feel good about herself, I have encouraged Frank to engage more in the relationship, and build the connection, without losing his sense of self.

It is our fourth meeting. Maxine is looking fantastic, and says she feels different, much more confident. She is no longer waiting for Frank to come home at night. She has good friends, and a social life. Ironically, now that she is beginning to differentiate, and is happier in her own skin, it is easier for Frank to be closer, as he doesn't fear being overwhelmed by her neediness. As he is increasingly able to be there for her, her neediness has diminished. They have moved away from the old vicious cycle; he used to keep his distance, which caused her to feel insecure and needy, which was unattractive to him and made him push her away, which made her more insecure. Now they are in a virtuous circle; she feels good about herself and does not need him to reassure her, whilst he no longer fears engulfment and being overwhelmed by her neediness. It has become easier for him to be close and loving, and she enjoys their closeness and feels good. The relationship dynamics are now mostly positive, and communication is good. It is time to think about sex. Frank is delighted – he would love more sex. Maxine has been the cautious one with apparent low desire, although I know that sometimes her libido is fine, but she is withholding sex. She agrees she feels ready to work on the sexual issues now that their relationship is better.

My aim is to help Maxine rediscover and connect to her desire, and so I ban sexual intercourse and masturbation. Maxine looks relieved, Frank is not so delighted! But I remind him that the intention is to get sex working well again, and they haven't been having much sex recently anyway. I set them on a programme of touching sensuously three times a week, for thirty minutes each time. They agree to do this naked, and to keep conversation to a minimum during the sensuous sessions. One will 'give' for fifteen minutes while the other 'receives', and then they will swap over. We agree that they will take it in turns to invite the other to the session. This allows them both to get used to instigating physical contact, which will help them later, when they want to invite each other for sex. In a way they are practising many of the skills of sexual communication without actual sex being involved. I tell them, "Don't worry, whatever happens, there is no failure, only feedback, meaning whatever happens in these touching sessions, it gives me information that I can work with in future sessions, and that will be useful. They are designed as an experiment to help move you both forward. I'm curious to see what happens and how they go."

They come back two weeks later. Frank looks proud, and tells me, "Well, I set the room up carefully. I made sure the heating was on, and it was warm. I put on a soothing CD in the background, and I even bought some rose oil, and used the aromatherapy burner that has been sitting in the cupboard. I read online that rose oil is good for the heart chakra. Then I invited Maxine, and she said she wasn't in the mood. I could've got cross at that – normally I would've, but I didn't. I was quite relaxed, and said if she changed her mind after supper, it was all set up and ready for us."

At this point Maxine breaks in, looking appreciative. "Actually that worked really well for me. I didn't feel pressurised, but it gave me time to get used to the idea, so actually, after supper, I felt ready for us to give it a go. But I felt very shy. It's a long time since we did anything like this."

"But it worked well, I thought," says Frank, as if making a statement, but then he looks over, to check with Maxine.

I am pleased by this, as I feel it shows progress. In the past Frank was focused on his own needs, and it didn't occur to him to check things out with Maxine, and I see this as a sign that he is giving more thought to her and the relationship. I comment on this. "I'm so pleased, Frank, that you didn't simply assume just now that it was good for you both, but checked it out with Maxine."

"Yes, I noticed that too," Maxine says to Frank, then continues, looking at me. "The sessions were pretty good for me."

We go on to explore what worked and what didn't. Maxine preferred being touched to touching Frank, and Frank was happy touching her. They had followed the instructions carefully and both had had equal time. The second session had also gone well. Maxine had also taken time to set the room up, and she had collected a range of items to touch Frank with, from a feather to a piece of fur and even an (unused!) green scouring pad. Frank says: "I loved the scouring pad on my back. I had my eyes closed, so I didn't know what it was, but I love having my back scratched. That is almost as good as sex! Though I wouldn't want her to use that everywhere!" he laughs.

Maxine goes on. "I found some new spots that were arousing for me." She looks at Frank. "I loved it when you rubbed your hands through my hair and scrunched my hair, that was... amazing... But the one place that was a revelation was when you kissed my ears... that was delicious. I wanted you to carry on for a long time – and my whole body was responding to you. You haven't kissed my ears before, not like that."

They had managed five sessions in the two weeks, and these had all gone well.

"Let's keep the ban in place for now," I suggest. They both nod, accepting this. I feel very pleased – this is really positive. I want to make sure that it continues this way, and that her desire for sex builds. They leave, looking much more loving.

Three weeks later they come back for another two-hour session. They arrive having had a row in the car. They tell me things have been more difficult since I last saw them. Maxine feels that Frank hasn't been as attentive and loving, and he feels that she has been nagging and nitpicking. We talk over the most recent row in some depth, to help them both feel heard. As each one speaks, their energy begins to shift. They look at each other more, and there are occasional smiles. The heavy mood gradually lifts.

I ask them, "Are you able to sort out all your rows like this?"

"No, this is fairly new. Normally we would just avoid each other for a few days, and the resentment would lurk."

"Well, the way you tackled it today is really impressive. I heard you both being open about your perspective, allowing the other one space to talk without interruption. You each acknowledged things you had done that hadn't helped, and there was a lot of honesty. If you can do this every time you argue, then it will make a huge difference."

They smile, clearly pleased with themselves. "I hadn't seen it like that," Maxine says. "All I saw was that we were having our usual problems again."

"But you are handling them a bit differently this time, and if you keep doing this, you will find that it changes the way you relate, and in a year's time you'll be back here saying you still row, but somehow you get over the arguments more easily and they damage the relationship less than they used to. If you handle each row with a tiny bit more awareness and proficiency than you did the last one, then slowly your newly-acquired skills will build up." The message I want to send is that making small incremental changes works. This will help them to notice the changes they are making and the things that are better, rather than thinking that nothing has changed.

When I ask about the 'sensuous touching' they both look awkward. Apparently they hadn't had so much time to do the exercises this time. Although they hadn't recognised why, as we talk about it Frank acknowledges that he had withdrawn because he felt that Maxine wasn't as available to him as in the previous weeks. "I was afraid of being rejected. Again."

Maxine had then felt hurt that he wasn't doing what they had agreed, and had taken it personally. Then she had pulled back too.

"I think what is needed here is to learn to be 'non-reactive to your partner's reactivity'[5]. This means, Frank, that when Maxine has a reaction to something you say or do, you have a choice: either to react to her reaction, or to step back and give space for Maxine to have her feelings, whilst you, Frank, concentrate on staying solid, grounded and composed. It is so easy for you both to wind each other up into tightly-coiled springs of frustration and anger (or fear and anxiety), which are then ready to explode like a hair trigger."

We had all recognised the habitual pattern: that when Maxine was demanding or rejecting, then Frank would pull back. But in this session, Frank was coming to realise that he also withdrew when he *anticipated* she was going to reject him. This was a further sign of his emotional fusion coming to the surface. He was not able to tolerate his own difficult feelings. Rather than risk Maxine rejecting him, and having to handle the sensations of pain that would cause, he pulled back, avoiding those feelings, but this meant that he sabotaged the 'touching' programme.

The session ends, and they leave, both determined to put what we had discussed into practice.

The next time I see them, they are back on track. The 'sensuous touching' has worked well, and both are feeling ready to take the next step, and move onto sexual intercourse. It is Maxine who asks: "I'm loving the touching, and I definitely feel ready for sex. My body is aroused, I am wet… and we both want to carry on." She smiles.

From here it was all pretty straightforward. They made love, and it was good enough. Sometimes it was very good, sometimes it was okay, and sometimes it was disappointing. But they were able to laugh when things didn't go as they might have hoped, and to talk it through. Maxine discovered that she was not so keen to initiate the sessions, but she was willing to let Frank know when she was 'available'. Sometimes she would let him know explicitly by telling him, "I have my sexy underwear on today". Other times she would give him a long, lingering kiss when he came home from work. They agreed that if either of them lit a candle in the living room, the other could take that as a 'readiness' signal. They were developing new ways of communicating about sex that were to stand them in good stead for many years to come.

I felt confident that the changes in their sexual life would last, because we had addressed the relationship issues first. Frank and Maxine were no longer so prickly and over-reactive with each other. The fundamental settings for their relationship had changed: from wariness to confidence, from doubt to trust, from fear to love and from blame to self-reflection. This had made a huge difference, and meant that even on the 'bad' days, when one or both of them were stressed, they somehow managed to be generous and kind.

Thoughts and Theory: The Confusion of Fusion

Lesson for people-pleasers: learn to put yourself first.
Lesson for authoritarians: learn to put others first.
Lesson for loners: learn to step forward and reach out.

Differentiation is a core concept that I find invaluable as a couples therapist. It is a route map for psychological health. Offering couple therapy that is underpinned by this model transforms a stressed and painful relationship into a calmer and more satisfying one. Another label for differentiation could be 'personal authority', and I will use these two terms interchangeably. The key distinction is that a differentiated person is able to make a self-directed choice *whilst remaining* emotionally connected to their partner. This is because they are clear about the difference between what they think and what they feel.

There are two opposing drives that all humans have to deal with. The first is the drive for individuality and autonomy, and the second is the drive for bonded intimacy and connectedness. Each person needs to find their relationship to these two competing drives. Many of us will favour one end of this spectrum. Like Frank, we may be good at making choices for ourselves, and prioritising our own needs (an over-developed First Position), but we do not fully consider the relationship and our partner's needs (a weak Second Position). Or, like Maxine, we prioritise the relationship and the emotional connection (too much Second Position), but we may not be able to meet our own needs (too little First Position). Finding a healthy balance between these two drives is the journey of a lifetime. The implications of getting stuck at one end of this continuum are profound. However, the couple are in a system together. When one person changes and shifts their balance, it will have a major impact on the other. It only takes one person to differentiate, and that will shift the dynamics of the whole relationship. These behaviours can be changed!

Although differentiation seems a straightforward idea, I have found it complicated to understand and even more challenging to actually live it. It has taken me a long time to really appreciate the deeper implications. The work I write about in this chapter initially came from Murray Bowen,[6] and was later developed by David Schnarch.[7] Interestingly, Bowen acknowledges that becoming differentiated is a lifelong process, and that 'total' differentiation is impossible to obtain!

Let's look at how the two drives of autonomy and connectedness work in practice. When Frank wants individuality, then Maxine feels rejected, and punishes him or pushes him away. Similarly, when Maxine wants closeness, it is easy for Frank to feel overwhelmed and thus emotionally cut-off from her. During therapy, as Maxine discovered her own authority, she found that she could give Frank space, and was surprised that she didn't feel threatened when he took 'time out'. As Frank differentiated, he discovered that he could enjoy closeness without feeling engulfed. The purpose of becoming differentiated, of taking full ownership of oneself, is to reduce our debilitating fears about being abandoned or smothered. Instead we are aiming for the increasing self-sufficiency *and* emotional connection that contributes to a healthy relationship.

The Pleaser, the Boss, the Loner and the Self-Developer

My adaptation of this work is a considerable simplification, into four possible roles we play in relationships. The *Pleaser*: this is Meg, at the start of her therapy. She is compliant, accommodating, and soothing. The *Boss*: Maxine fits this, and less obviously, Jamie. The Boss is controlling, dominating and stifling. The *Loner*: we see this in Frank with his patterns of withdrawing, avoiding, and emotionally cutting off. The Pleaser, the Loner and the Boss are all dominated by the feelings of those around them. Finally, we have the *Self-Developer,* who I also refer to interchangeably as the *Developer*: who is maturing, growing and holds the paradoxes of *my* needs and *our* needs, time *apart* and time *together*. The Self-Developer is the only healthy, differentiated role, who does not confuse their thinking with their emotions, nor do they have trouble differentiating their own feelings and emotions from their partner's. We see Jamie, Meg, Frank and Maxine each making steps as the Self-Developer at various points. The Pleaser, the Boss and the Loner are all roles of emotional fusion.

Traits of the Pleaser

In the role of the Pleaser we tend to: feel responsible for making our partner happy; compulsively seek acceptance; have poor boundaries; avoid confrontations; give up too much for our partner; yearn to receive but find it hard to accept love; have self-esteem that fluctuates according to our partner's view; and fear abandonment.

Traits of the Loner

In the role of a Loner we tend to: isolate to protect ourselves; feel threatened by healthy intimacy; keep people at a distance; appear not to care; avoid confrontation; be self-referential; need a lot of space; appear either arrogant or fearful; find it hard to receive any kindness or love; and fear engulfment.

Traits of the Boss

In the role of a Boss we tend to: need to control situations; dominate and manipulate in subtle ways; keep a score on who does what; be jealous or paranoid; make our partner feel unworthy; tease in a cruel way; not allow our partner to influence us; use guilt as a weapon; be generous so that our partner is in debt to us; make all the significant decisions; have a frightening temper; find it hard to receive any kindness or love; and fear losing love or losing control.

The healthy alternative: become a 'Self-Developer'

To become a Self-Developer we need to shift our focus away from others, and onto ourselves. The route to healing if we are other-dependent (a Pleaser, Boss or Loner), is to recognise that we do not have the power to change others, not even those we love. However, we do have the ability to change ourselves, and this is the action of the Developer, who is actively on the path of self-development. The journey towards the Self-Developer is to: see ourselves clearly; be honest with ourselves and others; own and honour our emotional wounds; know and accept our deepest feelings of shame, rage, terror, or grief; change any distorted or negative perspectives, beliefs and reactions; and have appropriate internal and external boundaries.

From feeling to thinking and back to feeling

To stand in your personal authority you need to be able to move from feelings to thinking, and back again, with ease. Not only that, but if you are to avoid being at the mercy of involuntary emotional reactions then you need to be able to discriminate between your *thoughts* and your *feelings*. This requires being able to fully experience and know your emotions. It also calls for the ability to switch to logical thinking in order to make sound decisions. The Pleaser, the Boss and the Loner are all dysfunctional roles connected to emotional fusion; they tend to become trapped in feelings, or in thinking, often confusing the two. Only the Developer is differentiated enough to clearly discriminate between thinking and feeling and move appropriately between the two.

Moving from Emotional Fusion

Emotional fusion, where we use other people to help us balance our emotional selves, is the opposite of differentiation. There are three ways that people typically regulate their emotional balance. They may disconnect and cut off. They might lean on their partner, relying on the other person to bring them back into balance. Or they dominate and control their partner, 'managing' the other person's responses, so that they don't say or do anything that will cause anxiety.

Alternatively, the Self-Developer will choose the healthy route, checking and self-confronting, then composing and rebalancing themselves. They remain clear about their own sense of themselves and their own value, whilst staying connected to the relationship.

Jamie and Meg

Often, an emotionally-fused couple will over-protect the other's feelings. Think of Jamie and Meg in Chapter 1. When Jamie first met Meg, *he felt strong when he was with her, in a way that he hadn't with other girlfriends.* Meg picked this up, and being the compliant one, she responded, *Meg sensed that Jamie was a bit unsure, and she instinctively wanted to protect him.* She wanted to bolster his self-esteem, and *reassure him.* On some level she recognised the dynamic: *she realised, with surprise, that she was more experienced than he was [sexually], – more confident in bed,* but then she modified her behaviour, *she held... back, reined in her exuberance, and concentrated on him and his pleasure.* By doing this, Meg was caretaking; regulating Jamie's emotional balance. She feared Jamie would not be able to handle her being *all* of herself, and so she diminished herself, presenting a smaller version. It was not so much that Jamie was overtly dominating, but that Meg had picked up that he couldn't handle much challenge. Not wanting to risk his disapproval, and being naturally compliant, she fitted in around him, allowing him to become the Boss in their relationship. Everything she did in the early days was in the service of 'harmony'. By habitually setting aside her choices, 'for the good of the relationship', Meg was people-pleasing. *In her quiet way, she let him know that he was a good lover, making little noises of pleasure.* It was all done from the best of motives, but together they had created an unsustainable system.

It was no surprise that a few years later Meg couldn't continue in this way. They could have separated at that point, but instead they made the brave choice of entering therapy. I explained to them that nothing had 'gone wrong'. Many of us are emotionally fused in our relationships. I certainly used to be, having started from the compliant end, the Pleaser. I reassured both Jamie and Meg that this was simply the beginning of the next level of their development, that they were moving towards a healthier relationship. They were learning about personal authority: differentiation in action.

The journey to becoming authentic

Meg needed to step into her authority and be more authentic: *"[Juliet] asked us how honest we are, and I realise I haven't been. I'm sorry."* She had to clarify what she wanted and be brave enough to speak it. *"I don't want us to split up… I want us both to work on it… I think there is a deeper level of love that we can reach."* She needed to check herself and think about where she was coming from, recognising what was important to her, her values and her principles. *"I need to take responsibility for being me. I need to speak my truth, and I need you to hear it and respond… I owe it to myself to get honest."* Then she had to commit to seeing this through, remembering those values, even when Jamie pressured her to revert to her old ways. This involved managing her anxiety about how Jamie would respond, as she spoke her truth, and not allowing herself to become overwhelmed by his reaction. *"It's been hell for me,"* Jamie complained. *"I feel like Meg is threatening our relationship."* When she was flooded by feelings, she had to breathe and compose herself, so that she could think logically. It was important that she focused on her own goal, separating *her* feelings from *Jamie's*, and trusted that *he* would be able to handle *his* anxiety. *"I do sometimes tell you what I think you want to hear rather than the whole, and sometimes brutal truth. I love you so much, I simply can't bear to hurt you."* She had to consider her responses to him, learning not to step in and rescue, to make it 'okay' for him. She recognised that she should not settle for less than she deserved. These were all important steps that someone from the Pleaser end of the spectrum needs to go through to differentiate.

Jamie's task, as the Boss, was to handle his feelings when he felt flooded by them. He needed to compose himself, so that he could keep thinking, staying flexible and open to Meg's needs. Once he began to see her needs as valid, he became willing to listen to her, be influenced by her, and sensitive to her truths. Learning to be more considerate, generous and giving, he became more co-operative, increasingly willing to check himself and confront his own behaviours, and more able to step forward and connect to her.

Frank and Maxine

Maxine was the Boss. Her pattern was to control Frank with her fury: *"If it wasn't for him, his lack of caring, his indifference, not to mention the fact that he flirts with other women. I know I can't trust him."* A Boss in a relationship with a Loner is the most challenging pairing. Maxine had described how she used to pursue Frank, because she wanted to talk about their problems. The more she tried to do this, the more he withdrew. When Frank avoided her, Maxine became more anxious, and pursued him all the more. Maxine reacted to her anxiety by seeking greater togetherness. She placed a high value on talking things through, which she saw as the best and only way forward. She felt rejected when Frank wanted to take time and space for himself. So she pursued and pursued him. Eventually, she would recognise that her strategy was not working, she would get angry, give up and go into a cold withdrawal, labelling herself as 'too demanding' and 'too critical'. Finally, she would blame Frank for not being able to handle closeness.

Whilst there was some truth in this, Maxine was missing the underlying issue, which was that she abandoned *herself*, and then made Frank responsible for her feelings of low self-worth. This meant that, in order to avoid her own painful feelings, she had to *control* Frank and manipulate him into approving of her. The less differentiated someone is, the more they will try to control others, either actively (by telling, criticising, or pressuring), or passively (by withdrawing, sulking, or playing the victim). She mistakenly thought it was Frank's job to make her feel desirable and worthy. She used blame, criticism, compliance, resistance and withdrawal to try to get from Frank the very thing that she was not giving to herself.

The path for Maxine, as the Boss, was to take back responsibility and step into her personal authority. She had to accept herself, "*I think there are some things I have been missing. Maybe I have been looking at things through a very dark lens and seeing problems,*" and learn to love herself. She had to let herself be influenced by Frank, rather than assuming she knew better than he did. This began to happen when I helped her to see that he really did love her, and that she had wilfully avoided seeing the signs. *Then I spot the shift beginning: as she opens to the possibility that maybe-he-does-love-her. A moment passes. She's looking down, but in that unseeing way that people have when they are remembering something. I wonder if she is thinking back over their recent past together? I hope that she is looking for signs that he does love her, signs that she may have missed before?* She also allowed herself to be influenced by me, and see another perspective when I pointed out that they were resolving their rows in a new way, *"I hadn't seen it like that,"* *Maxine said.* She became clearer about her goals and values, and more able to stand by them. She came to therapy with fewer expectations, and more to give to Frank and the relationship. She learned to control her behaviour, even when she couldn't regulate her feelings. This helped her to keep a better sense of proportion, so she was less likely to spiral into a negative state. As she composed herself, she was able to consider her responses, she lashed out at Frank less, and he felt safe enough to open up to her more. His flirting no longer threatened her, because her sense of self-worth was no longer tied to him or his behaviour.

For a Loner like Frank it was a different story. He may have initially seemed calm in response to Maxine, but if we had checked his physiological stress levels via a monitor that measured heart rate, body temperature and respiratory rate, I suspect it would have shown that his whole body was flooded with stress hormones. He had developed (as a child) a pseudo calmness – the uncanny ability to look cool on the outside, whilst sitting on a volcano inside. Frank thought of himself as self-reliant, not needing help, when actually he was disconnecting to avoid feeling his difficult emotions. Having never learned how to calm himself when stress levels were high, he was unable to tolerate any uncomfortable sensations in his body, so he sought emotional distance and space: *"It's impossible to talk to her when she is like this."* He withdrew and shut down, the typical pattern for Loners, who find it difficult to be vulnerable or needy. *"Maybe the kindest thing is just for me to go."* When Maxine shouted at him, he would covertly feel guilty, and withdraw further from her, often turning to his computer, or work for comfort. His emotional disconnection reflected a dilemma – the underlying fusion. It appeared to *solve* the dilemma, by reducing his anxiety at forming an emotional connection. But it also *created* a dilemma, because Maxine felt isolated.

Frank's cutting off from the relationship is just as much a sign of fusion as compulsive compliance. When thinking of fusion, it is easy to focus on the person who wants more togetherness. But the person taking space is doing so in reaction to their inability to tolerate closeness, and this is a reaction to the entanglement too. The higher your level of differentiation, the more intimacy you can handle.

If *I* had allowed the *we* of relationship, that would have forced *me* to no longer exist

The path to differentiation for Frank was to recognise his feelings, label them, and connect to them rather than avoid them. This was done initially in therapy, when I could help him to stay with the feelings and their accompanying physical sensations, and learn to recognise and name his emotions. As Frank said to me later on, "The way I used to see it, if 'I' had allowed the 'we' of relationship, that would have meant Maxine forcing 'me' to no longer exist." His strategy had been a defensive stance to keep her from annihilating him. As he learned to commit to himself and to his own development, and build healthier boundaries, he began to take Maxine's feelings or accusations less personally. He started to confront himself, and became more honest about his habits. He worked out how to concentrate on his goal, which was to stay with emotions and to be more present during discussions, without becoming overly rational. He learned to express his feelings and show his vulnerability, *"I was afraid of being rejected."* He recognised when he was starting to become flooded and hijacked. Then he would ask for space to cool down, agreeing with Maxine to meet again in forty minutes. During that time, he would compose himself, so that when they met up he was ready to carry on the discussion. The more he could deal with his anxieties around Maxine, the more he could commit to seeing this through, and connect to her, while staying open and fluid in himself.

Flooded by feelings

Meg, Jamie, Frank and Maxine were all protecting themselves by being the Pleaser, the Boss or the Loner. Meg was managing Jamie's feelings because, as is so typical in emotional fusion, she couldn't tell the difference between *her* thoughts and feelings, and *his*. This meant that she couldn't bear *her* anxiety at seeing *his* anxiety. She needed him to feel a certain way so that *she* could feel comfortable. Jamie, like Maxine, was getting cross because he couldn't handle *his* fear of abandonment. Frank was cutting off from Maxine because he couldn't handle *his* overwhelming feelings of staying connected to her emotionally. All were being flooded by their fusion and by their reaction to the other person. Each of them had to go through the challenge of learning to handle the anxious feelings (or feelings of fury) in themselves, feelings they had spent a lifetime avoiding.

The person who says, 'You make me angry', is giving the other person control over their state of mind, and this comment indicates that they have lost their sense of themselves. The Developer would say, 'I feel angry when you do X, and what I would like is…' (and here the Developer gives a suggestion for future behaviours).

We can all play all the roles

Although we each have a favourite role that we can easily slot into, we are all capable of doing all of them. So I can be compliant (the Pleaser), but I am also controlling (the Boss), and then when I don't get what I want, I get frustrated and withdraw (the Loner). We also change roles in different relationships. Jamie, for instance, was the Boss with Meg, but if he had been in a relationship with

Maxine, who was a stronger Boss than him, he would have slipped into the role of the Pleaser.

How to move from Loner to Developer

If I am a Loner and want to become a Developer, I need to work at being more attentive, and focussing on the connection with my partner. This will involve setting goals such as: be flexible and open to the needs of my partner; respect my partner's needs and wants; be sensitive to their truth; let myself be willing to be influenced by them and their ideas; be willing to give and be generous; be co-operative, and be willing to say, 'Yes'. As a Loner, I tend to be too detached, so the journey is to be more attentive and focus on connection with my partner.

How to move from Pleaser to Developer

If I am in the role of the Pleaser I am emotionally-fused, so in order to become a Developer I need to detach with love. My goals might be to: speak out for what I want and need; not to settle for less than I deserve; speak my truth even if it will be hard for my partner to hear or if it might lead to conflict; establish clear boundaries (for myself and for my partner); make choices based on *my* experience and beliefs; and be willing to say, 'No'.

How to move from Boss to Developer

If I am in the role of Boss, and am wanting control, then I need to step back and relinquish control. My goals might be to: be generous and not expect payback; see my partner as equal and not as less than me; let my partner make mistakes; accept influence; appreciate my partner's efforts; give genuine compliments; be co-operative; experiment with different ways of doing things; manage my feelings (e.g. jealousy).

Developing differentiation

Couples often come to therapy because they experience themselves as 'falling out of love'. But they may simply be falling 'out of fusion'! Or at least moving to the next stage of differentiation. These changes offer the chance to become a Self-Developer, to grow and step more fully into one's personal authority. Emotional fusion often feels like love, but generally it is a kind of pseudo intimacy where you are leaning on one another. True intimacy requires standing slightly apart, on your own, revealing new parts of yourself (that you may not have known about until now) and a ruthless honesty.

If you are hiding parts of yourself for fear of your partner's disapproval, using the other person as a crutch so you can face the world, or keeping yourself small because you fear that they won't be able to handle your full self, then you are emotionally fused. If you have to keep the peace because you cannot bear to see your partner unhappy, if you get infected by their moods which control your behaviour, or are giving in order to get, you are fused. If you stifle your partner by telling them what to do, looking after them so well that they can't manage without you, or cut off and withdraw, you are also emotionally fused.

True intimacy requires separation

To have genuine intimacy we need separation. The idea of fusion, two persons as one, is a romantic myth. True intimacy requires two distinct people, differentiated yet together, inter-dependent, choosing to be in a relationship, choosing to be together.

As Kahlil Gibran[8] says:

> Let there be spaces in your togetherness,
> And let the winds of the heavens dance between you.
> Love one another but make not a bond of love:
> Let it rather be a moving sea between the shores of your souls.

Fill each other's cup but drink not from one cup.

Give one another of your bread but eat not from the same loaf.

Sing and dance together and be joyous, but let each one of you
*   be alone,*

Even as the strings of a lute are alone though they quiver with
*   the same music.*

Give your hearts, but not into each other's keeping.

For only the hand of Life can contain your hearts.

And stand together, yet not too near together:

For the pillars of the temple stand apart,

And the oak tree and the cypress grow not in each other's
*   shadow.*

Chapter 3

Rakesh and Kim

It's not fair to rely on others to validate and define you. They'll get it wrong. Define yourself!

We learn so much from our families; they give us our first imprint of how to 'be' in a relationship. If you were lucky, and both your grandparents and your parents succeeded in developing themselves within their relationship, it is likely that you will have learned how to do that, too. If, however, you are like me, and your parents were not very successful at managing to maintain a clear sense of self *at the same time as* keeping an emotional connection with each other, then the chances are that this will not be your greatest skill either! I had a lot to learn about relationships. In my first marriage, which lasted ten years, I really did not understand what love was. As a child I had snuggled under the bedclothes as my mother read fairy stories to me. These told me that one day my prince would come and I would live happily ever after. As a teenager I had danced to the records that confirmed that once I was in love, I would never want to let the other person out of my sight, and we would be together forever. Yet I had also grown up watching my mother tiptoe around my father's sulking and moods, and learned that it was *my* job to ensure that he didn't get grumpy.

My strongest teenage memories are of my father's dark moods. I remember having three friends over one evening. My mother, who really wanted to be my sister, joined us for wine, cigarettes and loud music. By 9 p.m. we were lounging on cushions on the floor, with our shoes off, feeling very mellow and relaxed. A few hours later we heard the gate. Instant panic. Dad was home. We knew we had four and a half minutes before he'd come into the lounge – the time it took him to park his car in the drive. Four and a half minutes to get the room straightened, to put the cushions back on the sofa, our socks and shoes back on our feet, hide the wine bottle, and finish our drinks. When he walked into the room, there could be no-one sitting on the floor. We had to look as if we had sat, prim, proper and upright, on the sofa all evening. Four and a half minutes later, when he did come in, I held my breath. His displeasure leaked out, immediately dampening our high spirits, dousing us with disapproval. He didn't explode, but he sulked. For days. I think he felt threatened, and also jealous that he had missed some fun. He had been working; as a musician he was out, playing in concerts almost every evening. We had been enjoying ourselves, without him. I don't think he liked that. Yet it still puzzles me why he didn't like me bringing friends to the house. Maybe he felt that they threatened *his* family, and he worried they would take me away from him in some way. So, I learnt to be emotionally-fused, to tiptoe around men, to put my needs to one side to please 'the other', and to try to keep the peace in the house by being 'good', though somehow I never felt I succeeded in being good enough.

There is another pattern that I had, and frequently see in others. The more important my partner became to me, the harder it was to be fully myself. Or, perhaps more accurately, the more tempting it was to present the 'self' that I thought that my boyfriend (or husband) wanted to see. If I showed him only the part that he liked seeing, then he would love me, he would stay with me, and everything would be all right. We may even live happily ever after. Or so I thought!

Actually, as we have already seen (in Chapter 1 with Meg and Jamie), what happens in a long term relationship is that you probably won't be able to keep adapting forever, and at some point you will stand up for yourself and start to differentiate. This is what I saw happening when a gay couple, Rakesh and Kim, came for therapy. They were both in their late thirties, had some relationship issues and were not having much sex.

In our first session, Rakesh had spoken about how he'd begun training as an NLP practitioner, partly because his life felt a little hollow and empty, and because he was looking for a new challenge. Even in the first session it was clear that his newly-acquired knowledge had really stirred things up in his relationship with Kim.

It is our second session, and things have come to a head. Rakesh says, "I'm loving my NLP course, and it's making me realise that I am not the person I want to be. I am learning that I'm too concerned about what others think about me. I depend too much on what Kim says about me, and this determines how I feel about myself. And I don't like it. I was like that with my Mum. What she said went. If she said a hairstyle didn't suit me, then I didn't try it again. Or if she didn't like a shirt I didn't wear it. And if she said she didn't like one of my friends, then I thought she must be right.

"She was a kind of a goddess to me, and I assumed she was really wise. Now I am not sure that she was. In fact, on the workshops I have been doing I have realised, for the first time, that she actually craved love and appreciation from her own mother! I have got to the stage of seeing that I am doing this, seeking approval. I don't know what to do to change it. It is affecting our relationship, and we want some help. I want to be me, but to do that I have to work out who *I* am! That should be easy, but it isn't."

Several thoughts flash through my mind. The first: *How lovely to have a client who has reached this level of awareness about their problem, and who wants to change.* The second: *I wonder if they will make it as a couple, or if Rakesh will feel that he needs to step out of the relationship to 'find himself and get stronger', as he puts it.* The third thought: *This is such a common problem. This is another couple who have an emotionally-fused relationship, with poor interpersonal boundaries.* So many couples struggle with this issue. There is likely to be a lack of self-worth, alongside the need for approval. The common dynamic is that when one of them makes a move to autonomy, their partner will find it very threatening, and fear being abandoned. I wonder how Kim is doing. The fourth thought: I am going to need to be careful not to fall into the trap of being seen as 'the-wise-one-that-isn't-really-as-wise-as-he-thought-she-was-going-to-be', like his mother. I will watch out for that and sidestep it if I feel he is projecting that onto me. Finally, I remember what Schnarch says, that in every long-term relationship the couple will be at more or less the same level of differentiation as each other.[1] This means that when one moves into a more differentiated place, as Rakesh was beginning to do, the other will either change too, or, if they won't change (or can't change) then the relationship probably will not last.

I look at Kim. I find him hard to read. "How are you with this?"

Kim replies, "I know that something has to change. But we were doing okay, and now he has been on this course, I feel that I have lost him. Not only have we lost loads of *our* time over the past year – this course has been at weekends and he has done over twenty-five days – but he comes back all excited, raving about what he has learned. Sometimes I feel like he is trying out his new techniques on me, and I don't want to be his guinea pig – and now he is saying he doesn't want to need me in the way that he has in the past. I am worried he wants to leave."

Rakesh turns to Kim. "Actually it is simple. I love you. You are my husband. I am with you, and I want to be with you. I don't want to leave – but I am on a big journey, and I'm learning, and understanding a lot of things about myself, and I'm changing. I am excited about this new self-knowledge. I have discovered something that makes me happy. *Please* don't hold that against me. Don't stop me. I hate it that you want to hold me back."

I intervene, speaking to both of them. "It's interesting, because what Rakesh is saying is that he wants to be less dependent on your opinion, Kim, and he is recognising that in a healthy relationship you two would each be a separate and autonomous person, with a strong emotional connection, yet able to be fully your own self. Able to hold your own views, opinions, and your own 'shape', irrespective of what the other one thinks. So he *says* he wants that, and yet, Kim, when you have a reaction that Rakesh doesn't really like, he tries to stop you from expressing it. He *doesn't* want to hear it. So here we are. This is the work, right here, right now – we are doing it. So Rakesh, if you are going to wean yourself away from Kim's opinion, then you can start now. He has to be allowed to have his opinion – even, and maybe especially, if he disagrees with you."

Kim looks smug, and Rakesh looks chastened, and says, "I hadn't seen it like that. God. This is happening even more than I thought it was." He stops, then continues defensively, "but I don't like knowing that he doesn't want us to change, me to change."

"Then you are trying to control him, and his reactions." I pause, to let this land. I sense into Rakesh's skin… as Rakesh, I feel a bit bruised, but okay. Back as me, I think, *This is probably a good start. Everything I am saying is true. It is good to be aligning with Kim from the beginning. He seems to be the one who is being asked to change, and so is likely to be more reluctant. It is beneficial for him to feel me alongside him from the start of the session. I am glad that this has happened naturally. I hope that, if I can build the relationship with*

Kim now, that will allow me to say things that may be hard for him to hear, later on. I continue, "Rakesh, maybe you could soothe yourself, calm your anxiety, and let yourself and Kim really *be* separate, allowing him his own opinion even though you don't agree with it?"

"How do I do that?" Rakesh asks.

"Various ways, but one of the simple ones is to do what I call 'Seven-Eleven Breathing'. Breathe in and count for seven seconds, breathe out as you count to eleven. Do that a few times. The body relaxes on the *out* breath, so you want to ensure that you breathe all the way to the end of the out-breath. Right to the very end, before you breathe in. That will calm you down. You can also send yourself a positive message; mine would be something simple like 'you're doing okay', or 'he is entitled to have his feelings and I can have mine'. What might you say to yourself?"

Rakesh pauses, to consider for a moment, and then says, "All is good. Stay calm."

"Perfect," I respond. "And Kim, what might you use if you were soothing yourself?"

"I'm okay, you're okay. It comes from a book I read last year."

"That sounds great." Now I know that Kim has read at least one book on personal development, probably the book by Eric Berne called *I'm Okay You're Okay*, and I guess that if he has read this book, he might have read more. This is helpful.

"Being able to soothe yourself is a necessary skill for intimate relationships. I'd like you to really focus on practising this between now and next time we meet. Even when things are going well, let's say three or four times a day, will you take a few minutes out to soothe yourself, to do the breathing? To really focus on it. Are you both willing to do that?" They nod. "Self-soothing is probably the best relationship tool you can have. Rather than reacting when you find yourself getting caught up in each other's anxiety, you settle and compose yourself. So you become non-reactive to your partner's reactivity." I pause, letting this sink in. Then I add, "Being 'non-reactive to your partner's reactivity', which is a phrase from David Schnarch, means that when you find yourself feeling disapproved of, or you don't get the reaction you hoped for, you soothe yourself. When you realise that you have different opinions, and that disturbs you, you soothe yourself. If your husband is upset about something, it isn't *your* job to calm him down, he can do that for himself, *you* soothe *yourself*. You don't react. Then you won't overreact."

Kim says, sardonically, "That sounds pretty easy!"

"In a way it is simple, but it really isn't easy," I warn. "When you are in the middle of a row, and things are tense, you will tend to default to the old behaviours. What do you usually do in a row?"

Kim speaks up. "Well, I tend to leave the room. I don't like rows."

"And I find that bloody infuriating," Rakesh continues, "and I follow him. I want to talk things through, and I need to know that he isn't going to leave the relationship. I am always a bit scared of that."

"Great. That is a place you can work on. Rakesh, next time you row, try not following him. Let him walk away, maybe you walk away too, so that you are doing something different. And practise your self-soothing. You will need to have practised it before that, so you are able to do it even when things are really tense, in the middle of a row. If you try to do it for the first time during a quarrel, it won't work!"

They nod. "And Kim, next time you row, how would it be for you to stay there? Not to walk away. But to stand there, and to manage your feelings in that moment, to soothe your own tensions and anxieties?"

Kim looks doubtful. My heart opens to him. *How interesting*, I think, *I am more able to connect to him now. Maybe it is because he has become more vulnerable.* I feel into him, and he is nervous, unsure, and being swept along. I wonder if more information might help him, and give him some idea about how to do this. I smile, "I have devised a model to help couples to do this. It is a star, with five points. Each point is represented by a C. Check, Compose, Clarify, Commit, Consider. In the middle, underpinning all of these, is a B for Breathing. So the first thing you need to do is to breathe, which we worked on in our second session, and you have been practising the Seven-Eleven breathing at home. I think you both recognise that you relax a bit when you breathe out? Is that right?"

They nod.

"So throughout the different stages, remember to breathe! Then check yourself: to simplify things I am saying that there are four roles that we can fall into. Three of them are unhelpful, and we have talked about these in our sessions: The Pleaser, the Boss and the Loner. The Pleaser compulsively seeks approval from their partner, the Boss tries to control and stifle their partner, and the Loner cuts off. We talked about which one you are..."

Rakesh jumps in, "Yes, I recognise that I jump between the Pleaser and the Boss. I want his approval but I also want to tell him what he should feel."

Kim says, sounding long-suffering, "And I tend towards the Loner! We all know that."

"The second check is: 'Am I in the past or the present right now? In other words, has this issue tapped into something in my history? Is it loaded for me?'

"Having asked those, the next C is for Compose yourself. Take deep breaths, and breathe all the way to the end of your out-breath. This will help to soothe and settle you, so that both your thinking and feeling selves are available to you. Rakesh, you need to focus on thinking in these moments, as you can get railroaded by too many emotions. Whereas Kim, it is the feeling element that is more important for you. Here is an opportunity to stay with the feelings, even though they feel uncomfortable. Use your breath to compose yourself, and send yourself that message, 'I'm okay, you're okay'.

"So we have done Breathe, then Check, then Compose. The next C is for Clarify. What do you want from this communication? What is your goal? If it is a row, what are you aiming for? It could be 'to get my message across', or it might be 'to hear what Kim has to say, and to let him know I have heard him,' or 'to tell him what I think, whilst staying calm.'

"The next one is for Commit. Kim, this one is for you. If you are willing to try this out, this might mean that you experiment with *not* walking away from the row, but see what happens if you stay. And Rakesh, if he goes, you let him go, don't follow. Even if you desperately want to. Commit to letting him make his own choices. Manage your anxiety, and any other feelings. Pause, breathe, and compose yourself.

"The final one is for Consider. This is connected to being considerate, and doing what is needed for the good of the relationship. Neither of you are overly into the Pleaser, so it is okay for you to really pay attention to this. If I have a client who is an extreme people-pleaser, then I suggest they don't even think about this one, as they will tend to be over-considerate. But Rakesh, although you are a Pleaser at times, you also flip into the Boss very easily, so taking time to consider the best way to put your point across, in a way that Kim will be able to hear it, will be a good investment.

They look intrigued, and when I tune in to them, Rakesh is excited and Kim is feeling a bit more open, though still cautious. I continue, aware I am talking a lot, but I want to get the information over to them, to help them understand. I have spent years studying this process, and still find it complex and challenging to try and live in this way.

"If we have an emotionally-fused relationship, we tend to slip into the role of the Pleaser, the Boss or the Loner, as we all do to a greater or lesser extent. However, if we are to change, becoming a Self-Developer, then we are going to have to commit to staying with lots of moments of anxiety and feelings that we have avoided in the past. When we start to do things differently, it will feel strange at first. And difficult. Really, really difficult. And you won't change overnight. You will probably find that you have more rows for a while. Sorry Kim!

"The benefit, however, is that your relationship will get stronger, as you become more able to be yourselves, without being pulled into reacting to each other. You won't have to avoid your partner, or put him down to feel good about yourself. You'll discover that you can compose yourself and *contain* your anxiety, so it is not spilling all over the place. You won't have to control or manipulate each other. You won't be reluctantly giving way to keep the peace. After a while, you will have a new level of confidence, and feel good about yourself, perhaps a greater sense of self-respect. You will be able to handle the balance between *your* needs and the needs of the *relationship*. You will see each other as individuals, know that you are different, and appreciate each other's strengths and weaknesses. You may even realise that your differences can enrich your relationship.

"What's more, something interesting often happens over time. Rather than keeping the conflict *between* the two of you, and trying to force your husband to adapt or accommodate you, you will start to bring the conflict *into yourself*. Then, the first step you take when there is a difficult situation is to confront *yourself*, rather than *the other*. So that first C, of Check yourself, becomes *Confront* yourself. When you get to this stage then the amount of conflict will reduce. As you become more aware of your own shortcomings, inevitably you'll become more forgiving of each other's foibles. You won't blame each other so much. And you'll learn to talk from the heart, instead of being armoured-up."

They are both nodding.

"And remember, stepping back from getting caught in each other's anger and anxiety, and learning to become two separate people often has a really good effect on your sex life. Sexual desire seems to depend on difference and separation. With emotional fusion you are like Siamese twins who share feelings – and you have to keep the other one calm because you can't handle the anxiety *you* feel at *their* anxiety. When you have differentiation in the relationship, then you can each let the other have his feelings without being 'infected' (and affected) by those emotions. You are separate, but you still have a strong emotional connection. You are willing to be seen for who you are, because you accept who you are. That is when the sex gets really good, and that is what real intimacy is about. One of my clients once said to me, 'Intimacy stands for 'into me I see'. You have to like yourself enough to let another person see into you. And that includes in the bedroom."

Kim is leaning forward now. "Mmm. That sounds more like it!"

"Yes, but it is not a quick journey. It will take some time, but you've already started. You are here. You have decided to work on it. And when we look back in four or five months' time I imagine you'll be surprised how far you have come. Although there will be many rocky moments on the way, the journey is worth taking."

I tend to predict some problems, so that if they hit them they don't become despairing and think it isn't working. Also, I see the problems as a part of the journey. "I've talked a lot this session, sorry about that! Just remember, relationship problems are a sign that you are normal. We all reach the power-struggle stage of relationships at some point. There is nothing going wrong. It's what happens to everyone. And now you have an opportunity to make your relationship healthier. I will be interested to see you next time, to hear how it has gone for you both."

Rakesh and Kim: Two Months Later

... the anger of a thousand yeses
in place of a solitary no.
William Ayot[2]

Rakesh and Kim have been coming for therapy every two or three weeks, and as I predicted there have been ups and downs, and they have been arguing more. Kim has stopped walking away from arguments, so they have been standing and shouting at each other, which both have found distressing. They have been feeling that the relationship was getting worse, and I was very relieved that I had warned them about that possibility.

I trust that if I help each of them to continue to develop their own sense of self and to learn to self-soothe and compose themselves, they will find a new equilibrium with each other soon enough. I see this stage – of them standing up for themselves – as a really positive sign. They are showing me that they are changing, by not saying 'yes' when they really mean 'no', being reluctant to compromise in a way that might lead to later resentments, and staying longer with their painful feelings. Having started to stand up for themselves, and to ask for what they want, they now need to learn about negotiating and about how to argue in non-toxic ways. I realise that they do not know about *healthy* anger, so, at our next meeting, I talk them through Sue Parker Hall's[3] work on anger.

"It's important to distinguish between anger and rage," I say. "Parker Hall says that anger is expressed in less than five minutes, whereas rage can take much longer – hours or even days – to express. With anger, we can both think *and* feel. With rage, rational thought is impossible."

Rakesh responds, "Then what we are doing is rage. It never takes five minutes... once we start, then we just keep going. It gets bloody."

"Do you mean that you are violent?" I check.

"Never physically, but emotionally, verbally, yes."

"Parker Hall says that if there was no one to teach you how to acknowledge and handle your feelings when you were a child, then you will push those feelings underground because they feel overwhelming. They go into a 'rage pot' which gets fuller and fuller, and eventually starts overflowing, as the uncontained feelings burst out inappropriately."

"That is me," Rakesh says. "My mum had post-natal depression and four other children. She didn't know how to soothe her own feelings, let alone help me with mine. In a way it was as if she wasn't really interested in us. She was either depressed or too busy. I guess I grew up hungry for her love, wanting more, wanting her approval. Sometimes she would give me attention, and that was lovely. I remember those moments. Yet sometimes it was as if I wasn't there. And later on, when she recovered from her depression, she got busy at work. She was never good at acknowledging how she felt."

Then Kim chips in. "I guess my mum was too young. She was only sixteen when she had me, and her father had been a violent man. He didn't know how to handle his anger. Mum had learned from him and she was quick to anger. She could lash out too. That's why I have walked away in the past. I hate it when people are shouting. I feel afraid. The last few weeks have been horrible for me."

"With a history like that, I can see it would be terrifying for you," I agree. I pause. "There is another piece to this rage stuff

94

too. Parker Hall separates out 'hot rage' and 'cold rage'. 'Hot rage' is when the feelings boil over, in a way that is disproportionate to the situation, and I think that describes you at times," I say, looking at Rakesh, who nods. "As opposed to 'cold rage', when you might say *I don't feel angry*, and your rage is denied. People with cold rage often feel numb, depressed or have other symptoms. Or they may not be feeling much at all, they might have disconnected from almost all their feelings and emotions. Parker Hall would say that rage – be it hot rage or cold rage – is not an emotion. She calls it 'a defence mechanism, evoked when a person is overwhelmed by their experience and unable to integrate it.'"[4]

Rakesh says to Kim, softly, "Darling, I think you have that cold rage...?"

Kim looks irritated, but then reluctantly concedes. "Maybe."

I continue. "She describes anger as much gentler, almost benign."

"Benign!" exclaims Kim.

"She says anger *is* an emotion. I often name this *healthy anger*, though the point that Parker Hall makes is that *all* anger is healthy; it is *rage* that is unhealthy. The first sign of anger might be quite a small signal. It is what you feel when someone steps over your boundaries, or violates you in some way, such as forcing their opinion onto you. Remember, in anger you are able to think *and* feel at the same time. You can find the right words. You speak with assertive authority, but you are not aggressive. You say what you need to say in a few minutes, and you are respectful of the other person. Healthy anger is used to solve a problem in the here and now, and you don't bring up baggage from the past."

"Golly." Rakesh says.

"I have a way of working with these early childhood issues that I find effective. I use a method called the Pesso Boyden System Psychomotor (PBSP).[5] It is a therapeutic method that literally changes the way people feel about their past, and how they respond in the present. This is done by using symbolic figures, to 'antidote' the things that were less-than-ideal in our real history."

They look open to hearing more. "We do this by bringing in an imagined 'Ideal Figure', who would have been there in the way that was needed when you were a child.

"When things go well, we learn about composing ourselves, self-soothing from our mothers.[6] If a baby is distressed and anxious, opiate and oxytocin levels drop which causes physical pain. That in turn releases the stress hormones – adrenaline and cortisol. At this stage, mother and baby are so closely connected that the mother's neurochemicals impact the child." I slow down a bit, because I want them to really hear this. "When a mother soothes her baby *she* releases calming oxytocin, and the oxytocin levels in the baby increase too. The baby soon forms 'default soothing pathways' in both their brain and their body. These will help them for the rest of their lives.

"However, if the mother is not available, maybe she is depressed, distracted, drunk, or doesn't respond to the infant quickly enough, then the default pathways that form are based around anxiety, panic and stress. So the baby grows up predisposed to getting stressed, and will have difficulty soothing, both as a child as an adult." They look slightly dazed. I carry on. "Luckily, we can attend to this early patterning using PBSP. I hear from so many different clients that using the Ideal Parents has literally changed how they feel about, and respond to, stressful situations."

Kim and I start to think about what he would have needed as a child. Rakesh sits, watching, whilst Kim creates an Ideal Mother who would have been twenty-six (rather than sixteen) when she gave birth to him. He loves this idea. He begins to realise that by using this technique he can create, in his mind, the perfect start for himself. He decides that his Ideal Mother would have been Italian. He realises that one way to think about his Ideal Mother is to have her do the exact opposite of his real mother. He says, "It is important to me that my mother…"

"Your *Ideal* Mother," I gently correct.

"Yes, okay, it is important to me that my Ideal Mother has a loving Ideal Father who doesn't ever lash out."

I encourage him to put this back in time. Kim imagines himself as a child, with his Ideal Mother standing on his left, behind him, with her hand resting on his shoulder. Then Kim places *her* Ideal Father (his Ideal Grandfather) beside but slightly behind his Ideal Mother. All of this is in his mind's eye: he is imagining himself as a child aged ten. Kim, smiling broadly, says, "We all would have lived in Italy in the countryside, on a farm. I see Italy as a place where children are welcomed, loved and cherished." His Ideal Grandparents (his Ideal Mother's Ideal Parents) would have lived nearby, reached a ripe old age, and would have supported her emotionally. "They would have loved to have me over to stay, and would have been regular visitors at the farm," he says, sounding excited. I can see he is really getting into this now. "The whole extended family would have been good communicators, able to express their emotions appropriately – especially anger."

Kim's Ideal Father would have been around as he grew up (his real father was away a lot) and he would have enjoyed his children (Kim's real father had had very little time for him). Kim imagines his Ideal Parents together, looking lovingly at each other. He describes them having had an affectionate, tender and rewarding relationship, so that he could have grown up seeing adults who were warm and loving, and who talked things through together when there were problems. He leans back, and sighs contentedly as he imagines both Ideal Parents snuggled up on a sofa together, with him in the middle.

Rakesh and I can both see how much satisfaction and pleasure Kim feels as he imagines them being there with him. So I let Kim know that I am going to leave him to embed the experience with his new Ideal Family, and I shift my focus to Rakesh.

Rakesh imagines having an Ideal Mother who was happy. His real father had left when he was only a few months old, so he creates an Ideal Father who was present, both for his mother and for himself, from the beginning of his life. When he imagines his Ideal Parents hugging, tears roll down his face. "If my real father had stayed," he says, "it would have made a huge difference to how my mother would have coped." Describing his Ideal Mother, he shapes a woman who he can really believe in. She is naturally cheerful, optimistic and robust. She would have bounced back if there had been challenging times. His Ideal Mother would have known all about soothing a baby, and, as he describes it, "She would have been a really warm and loving Earth Mother who I could have trusted to *consistently* be there. She would not have needed to work when I was young." He decides that she would only have had two children, so that he would not have had to compete for her attention.

As Kim and Rakesh create their Ideal Parents, fleshing them out in a way that makes them believable, I see their bodies respond. Their faces relax, loosening out so they look younger. Their breathing changes and deepens and they sigh, suggesting that they are letting go of old tensions. I find my own body relaxing too as the shifts and changes release old hurts for them. When they say, "That would have been wonderful," I can see by their inner glow that they are living into that new possibility, and experiencing these new, pleasurable feelings right now.

By helping them to plant the image of these Ideal Parents firmly into their past, and linking that image with the sensations that they are feeling *now* in their bodies, the PBSP process helps Rakesh and Kim to imagine that they could have felt like *this* at a younger age. My aim is to help them create a credible, lasting experience that both provides a change in itself, and becomes the foundation for them to build on. The longest lasting changes occur when the weight of new, positive memories outweighs the historical accumulation of negative memories. Then Rakesh and Kim will find that they don't get so irritated, that they can handle the anger in more positive ways, and they will hopefully have more and more moments of spontaneous happiness.

Thoughts and Theory:
The Model of Five Star Conscious Relating

When your partner gets upset or angry you can either react
automatically, or choose to respond wisely.

I created the Five Star Conscious Relating model to help us to stay centred, even when things get difficult in an intimate relationship. This model is about not reacting in your customary automatic way, but instead having a conscious response to your partner.

Five Star Conscious Relating

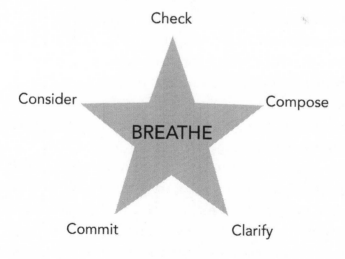

© Juliet Grayson

Breathing is the core, and lies at the centre. It is accompanied by five different tasks: Check, Compose, Clarify, Commit and Consider. Earlier, in Chapter 2, I wrote about the challenges of making a self-directed choice whilst staying emotionally connected to your partner; in other words, being me *and* being in a relationship. The Five Star Model provides us with the tools to do this.

Breathe

At the core of the Five Star Conscious Relating model is our breath. This is a natural resource, and an in-built stress reliever. Breathing happens day and night without us thinking about it. We can breathe well, or poorly, but those of us who live in an almost permanent state of mild anxiety or stress are likely to breathe in a very shallow way, yet usually we are completely unaware of this. For most of us, our everyday breathing is easy, until our partner pushes our 'hot buttons', when we automatically react. We get stressed, our heart rate increases and breathing becomes shallow. But the good news is that we can *choose* to override the automatic system, and breathe more slowly and deeply. Changing our breathing changes how we feel.

Whenever we are stressed our breath is naturally fast and shallow. Stress, anger and fear activate our sympathetic nervous system – which is also known as the fight, flight or freeze system. Shallow breathing puts less oxygen in the bloodstream, which leads to an increase in muscle tension, which in turn can make us feel more anxious and uptight.

I remember one client who had been sent to boarding school when he was seven-years-old. It was such a shock to his system it was as if, from that day on, he only dared to take shallow breaths. As he grew up, he noticed that he found it very hard to identify what he was feeling. He hadn't realised that he was shallow breathing, and through this he was protecting himself, as all of us can, from experiencing his emotions.[7] Forty years later, when we worked together on a sexual issue, and I re-introduced him to deeper breathing, he said, "Golly. I don't think I have breathed like this since I was six." As he changed his breathing patterns, he became more aware of his feelings, learning to both distinguish between his different emotions, and to name them.

By deliberately slowing our breath, and focusing on long out breaths, we can quickly shift our body from the fight or flight mode (sympathetic nervous system), to the rest and digest system (the parasympathetic nervous system) which is part of the body's relaxation and soothing toolkit. By breathing in to a count of seven, and out to a count of eleven (as Kim and Rakesh learnt to do in Chapter 2) we send our body a message that it is safe to relax. If we go a step further, and encourage our belly to move in and out as we breathe, then our breathing will drop from the upper chest (which is related to higher stress levels), to the diaphragm area, and we will calm down even more. As we breathe out, our heartbeat slows down, and our body relaxes. We may even begin to feel safer. We are sending a message to our body, via the speed and quality of our breath, which says 'there is nothing for me to worry about right now'.

The more we practise this, the more we will be able to utilise breathing techniques in times of stress, as a form of quick relaxation, to soothe and settle ourselves in just two or three breaths. It is so simple, yet many of us are unaware that we can use our breathing to change our state of mind!

Check yourself
There are two aspects to this rigorous self-checking. The first is to establish, "Today, am I behaving more in the role of the Pleaser, the Loner, the Boss or the Self-Developer?" The second is to establish, "Am I operating in the present or reacting to my history?"

The First Check: The Pleaser, The Boss, The
Loner and the Self-Developer
Those of us who get caught for extended periods in the role of the Pleaser, the Loner, or the Boss tend to be overly caught up in our

partner's reactions in a dysfunctional way. If my sense of self and my self-esteem are largely based on what my partner will support and validate, then I am set up to be a helpless victim. I will be too easily affected and influenced by his or her moods and desires. It is easy to see how this works with those of us who are often in the role of the Pleaser. However, it may seem surprising that this is also true for those of us in the role of the distant Loner. We may not *seem* to be overly affected by our partner's reaction, but when we investigate the underlying motivation of those of us who are Loners, we see that we are avoiding intimacy and connection. This may be because the influence of our partner (or for some, even the idea of *having* a partner who *might* affect us) is too much for us to bear, so we, the Loners, feel that we *have to* take space, as a survival strategy. Those of us in the role of the Boss are also other-dependent, often struggling with the influence that our partner has on us. Our solution is to stifle and control our partner, to attempt to manage our own stress levels.

It is only those of us in the role of Self-Developer who have a sufficiently strong sense of self to be able to be both fully emotionally connected to our partner, *and* able to maintain our sense of ourselves. We do not confuse our own thinking with our own feelings, *nor* are we overly infected with our partner's moods and emotions. We can clearly recognise what feelings belong to us, and what feelings belong to our partner, so we can remain open to them. Remember, we all move around all of these roles, in different relationships, on different days, or even within the length of just one conversation, although most of us have one role that we default to in times of pressure, anxiety, or anger. It is when we get caught up in just one role most of the time, that it is dysfunctional.

The Second Check: Am I in the past or the present right now?
The underlying question is, "Am I conscious, or am I caught?" Am I conscious, fully present in the 'here and now', or am I 'caught',

re-enacting or responding to my old historical patterns? If we are having a disproportionate reaction to something, then it is probably tapping into our history. Ask yourself, "Does this remind me of how I felt with my mother, my father, or a previous partner?" "What age do I feel right now (e.g. adult, or six years old)."

As I write this I am taken back to a moment in a thunderstorm thirty years ago, outside Pizzeria da Guido, in Valeggio-sul-Mincio in Italy, where I was living and working. We had the most marvellous view, looking over fields in the middle of the countryside. I was standing outside when there was a sudden deluge; the rain bucketed down, and I got completely soaked through. I felt furious, and I remember stamping my foot, in a *complete* rage, screaming at R, my first husband, "I told you this would happen! I told you!" I have no recollection of what the row was about, but I remember feeling about three-years old as I stamped my foot!

If we confront ourselves, thus catching the moment when we are reacting more to our own history than to something that is happening in the 'here and now', then we can start by taking a few deep breaths. Then we might verbally acknowledge that our reaction may be larger than we would normally expect for this situation, and that the issue is (or could be) 'loaded' with our history.

We saw how Kim's history affected his ability to handle conflict. Kim had learnt from his mother that anger was dangerous. When he was in any kind of disagreement with Rakesh, his little-child self was telling him that it was not safe. Kim was not in an 'adult' place when he was walking away from those rows.

Meanwhile, Rakesh had lacked love and approval as a child, and so his 'inner-child' was desperate for that from Kim. But actually, Kim's reassurance would never fill the gap left by Rakesh's childhood, because Kim was not in the right kinship relationship. Again, Rakesh hadn't been responding from his full adult self, but those interactions with Kim, where Rakesh was looking for more, were loaded with his historical deficits.

Compose yourself

It is so easy, as soon as our partner presses our 'hot buttons', to find ourselves exploding or pulling away. Neither of these responses will help us to achieve our goals. So it is best to settle ourselves, breathe, and stay calm. Learning how to soothe, and settle oneself (like Rakesh and Kim earlier in this chapter) is an invaluable skill for couples. This can be done in the moment, by slowing and deepening our breathing, being sure to breathe out to the very end of the out-breath. It is even better if you accompany this with positive self-talk (any phrase that calms you, such as, 'Just relax' or, 'You are doing fine'). Kim's was, 'I'm okay, you're okay.' Rakesh preferred, 'All is good, stay calm.' Being unruffled enables us to access both our thinking and our feeling so that we can move easily and appropriately from one to the other and back again. We can only do this when we are composed.

If we have got to the point of being flooded with an emotional response, then it can be helpful to negotiate a break to calm down. I suggested this to Maxine in Chapter 2, as she would often wind herself up and up into a state of fury and wrath. This time out allows the neuro-chemicals related to our fight and flight reaction to settle back to equilibrium. We should take a break of twenty to thirty minutes. It is important, during this time, to avoid fuelling the outrage by saying things such as: "He *always* criticises me like that," or "I hate it when she treats me with such contempt." Instead, do something calming or distracting such as going for a walk, taking vigorous exercise or listening to relaxing music.

John Gottman, an American psychologist who is known for his work on marital stability and relationship analysis, confirmed the benefit to couples of taking a thirty-minute break when things were getting tense.[8] He had a 'Love Lab', a hi-tech apartment that was wired up with microphones and cameras. Couples would spend a few days there, as if on a short break. Whilst in the Love Lab participants wore monitors to check their physiological functioning such as blood pressure, respiratory rate, and the amount they nervously 'jiggled'. He observed that when a person's heart rate reached over one hundred beats per minute they simply couldn't hear what their partner was saying, even if they were willing to try. So Gottman, as part of his study, would interrupt couples just as they were beginning to argue, telling them that the equipment needed adjusting. He asked the couple not to talk about their issue, but to read a magazine for half an hour. He discovered that when his couples started to talk about their issue again, their heart rates were significantly lower and their interaction was much more positive and productive. Having a break of thirty minutes really helped them to manage their composure, which improved their relating.

Clarify your goals

Once we have honestly *checked* ourselves, what role we are playing, and whether this issue is current or loaded with our history, and we have *composed* ourselves, then we can think about the next thing, which is to *clarify our goals*. It is important to know what we want. Often in a challenging conversation we lose track of our original intention. Imagine two people who both order a taxi. One person doesn't know where she wants to go; so when she gets into the taxi, and the driver drives off she could end up anywhere! The second person also doesn't know where he wants to go, but he knows where he *doesn't* want to go. He tells the driver, "I don't want to go to Oxford or to Ascot." It is no surprise that he too fails to arrive where he intended to go, which was Heathrow.

When things are getting sticky, it is good to clarify what we want. If our goal is to shout at our partner and lose our temper, then go ahead! Enjoy having a rant! However, if we want to reach a decision about some disagreement, or negotiate about something, then it helps to be really clear and focus on achieving that goal. We shouldn't get hijacked by strong emotional reactions, either our own or those of our partner. As with many of our habitual patterns, we need to practise when life is going well and not expect ourselves to get it right when life is difficult. So, every day, think, "What do I want today?" Or even, "What do I want right now?" Before every conversation it is wise to take a few moments to clarify the goal, and to focus.

We saw Meg take her courage, and focus on her goal, in Chapter 1, when she said, "I want more fun in our relationship." We discovered that she was thinking of having more fun in a variety of ways, ranging from hiking through to a better sex life.

It is worth remembering that in any negotiation, our partner is much more likely to give us what we want if we dovetail outcomes. A dovetail joint is a woodworking joint, with interlocking tails and pins. We are most likely to get what we want when there is some advantage for our partner too, some benefit that they receive when they give us want we want. For example, "Can I use the car tomorrow to go for lunch with my girlfriends and, if it helps you, then on the way I could pick up the hammer that you wanted to borrow from Pete." Please note, that someone who is strongly in the role of a Pleaser will tend to over-give anyway, so they should not focus on dovetailing outcomes. This process will be more important for the Loner and the Boss.

Commit to seeing this through

This is about committing to seeing *this* moment through: *this* argument or *this* discussion. If we are a Loner who avoids conflict, we commit to staying present and not walking away (like Kim). If we are a Pleaser we commit to tolerating the complex and painful feelings we will have when we stand up for ourselves (like Meg). Or we may have to tolerate the discomfort of our partner doing something different (like Jamie). New behaviours feel risky, and can bring up strong feelings – this may feel dangerous to a part of us. We need to commit to our breathing, to settling ourselves down, and allow our partner to have their reaction, without reacting back.

It is worth noting here that, in another study, John Gottman[9] found that 69% of couples' problems are in the category that he called a 'perpetual problem'. A perpetual problem occurs when there is a fundamental difference, for example in lifestyle needs or in personalities. The couple will return to this issue or issues over and over again, year after year. Gottman found that the best way to handle these recurring problems was not to try to solve them, as on the whole they were not solvable. Instead, his advice to both parties was to remain open and be willing to talk the problem through, again and again, with humour, tolerance and affection. He suggested working out the areas of the problem where there is no flexibility whilst also defining the areas where there is room to yield, and then devising a temporary compromise that honours both people's dreams. The commitment to keep the dialogue open for further discussion seems to stop it from escalating to a grid-locked situation where everyone feels frustrated and cross.

Consider your reply

The first four tasks have been focused on us. We have *checked* ourselves and our part in the issue. We know which role we are coming from (Pleaser, Boss, Loner or Developer). We have thought about the timescale we are in (present day, or the past). We have *composed* ourselves, so that we are quiet (or quieter!) inside. We are *clear* about what we want, and what the benefit will be to us, to our partner and to the relationship. We have *committed* to see this through, to find a solution, or to accept that there is no solution, and to keep on talking it through whenever necessary.

Now the focus shifts onto our partner. But this time it is not from a place of other-dependence where we are reliant on their approval, or trying to keep them calm in order to avoid our own difficult feelings, but rather from a place of *consideration* and generosity. This is about conscious relating, and giving consideration to our partner. We think about what we are doing and saying, and how we are doing and saying it.

People communicate through three channels: the words, the tone of voice, and the body language. So if someone says, 'I am really fascinated by what you are saying,' in a bored voice tone, whilst sending a text on their mobile phone, we will take it either as an amusing ironic comment on their level of interest, or be deeply hurt that they don't care. Mehrabian[10] says that the words only account for 7% of the message received, whilst the tone of voice is 38% and the body language 55%. These percentages point to a truth, that the majority of our communication is not *only* carried by the words, but is also carried by the *way* in which we say them. A slight change of voice tone changes the meaning entirely. Our body language can easily undermine what we want to say. If we are conscious of our communication, we will pay attention not only to what we say, but also to how we say it, to ensure that our communication is congruent and aligned, with the words, voice tone and body language all sending the same message.

When we are consciously communicating, and considering our partner, then we bring the best of ourselves to the discussion, or disagreement. This means that we don't just act out and shout, or, in a passive aggressive way, sulk and punish our lover. Instead we stand in our grounded selves, and work alongside them to explain our thinking, whilst seeking to understand *theirs*. We let them know we have heard them, by repeating back their key points. A useful saying from NLP is: the meaning of the communication is the message that is *received*, not the message that is *intended*. In other words, if I intended to be kind, but my partner heard my comment as sarcastic then it is *my* responsibility as the sender of the message to have a second (and possibly third) attempt, to express myself clearly, with a suitable voice timbre and tonality, so I am not misinterpreted.

If our partner does react to something, it is important that we remain calm and composed, not reacting to their reaction. We do our best to ensure that our thoughts and decisions are considered, governed not only by our rational thinking but also our intuitive heart and our instinctive gut. This is a particularly important one for those of us in the role of a Boss or Loner.

The paradox

An extra thing to consider is that in every case the way forward depends on the character of the individual. If I have spent the last forty years locked into the role of the Pleaser, then the final step of this model (considering my partner) needs to be taken lightly, as my tendency has been to be over-considerate and then to get resentful. This is where the 'Check yourself' step is so important. Recognising I am a Pleaser, I have to work on stating my needs, and expecting my thoughts and ideas to be taken into account, and giving myself permission to ask for, and receive, what I want.

In the same way, if, like Kim, I am stuck in the role of Loner, then I owe it to myself and to the relationship *not* to take time out when composing myself, as that is my default pattern – and for Kim it is an avoidance and not a healthy option. Instead, Kim's challenge is to make a commitment to stick with the discussion, and tolerate his own challenging feelings.

All relationships are in a state of dynamic equilibrium. My experience over the last twenty-five years of working with couples (not to mention more than forty years of my own experience of intimate relationships) is that there is often a rocky phase as the equilibrium shifts to a more conscious relationship, and the dynamics are re-balanced. As each of us increases our emotional maturity, we reach a higher level of differentiation and improved functioning. We become less likely to be triggered by our partner or other stressors, and more rational even in challenging situations. However, all this depends on us doing our personal development. If we are not willing to do the necessary psychological work, then we are at the mercy of our past, and we will be marching to someone else's tune.

Chapter 4

Sheila

If you want to be unconditionally loved, have a baby or buy a dog!
Don't expect that from your partner.

"What I yearn for, what I most want in the world is simply to be accepted and loved for who I am. Unconditionally. Is that so much to ask?" Sheila's blonde, wispy hair frames her rounded face, and she looks like a forlorn and vulnerable six-year-old. Her loose black blouse emphasises her paleness and fragility.

Sheila has come to therapy on her own. She is very keen to find a relationship. "I've been looking for years! But we don't often make it past six weeks," she says. "They start off keen, and then something happens, and they start to let me down." That is when she asks me about unconditional love. "Is that so much to ask?"

The brutal answer to her question is *Yes! It is too much to ask.* But I don't want to say that straight away. I am curious to see what is behind this, and the fact that I can see the six-year-old in her gives me a clue. My hunch is that she is bringing her neediness to relationships.

"I'm on my own and I just don't seem to be able to find a partner who will love me. I mean, *really* love me," she explains, biting her lower lip.

My own first marriage had been based on my misunderstanding of what love is, and I could really relate to her question. It has taken me many years of thought, research, and my own personal development to realise that unconditional love is something that one *should* get from a *parent*, but that one should *not* expect from a *partner*. I find it ironic that those two words are so similar. Jumble the letters up, add one in for luck and you move from p-a-r-e-n-t to p-a-r-t-n-e-r. Many people want to slip from a parent to a partner without really noticing the difference, hoping to feel the same kind of love from a partner that they should have received from their mother and father. This loads so many inappropriate expectations onto their adult sexual relationship. Although they don't realise it, in many cases they are hoping to satisfy the unmet needs from their childhood. I think to myself, *I wonder if this is the territory that Sheila and I'll be exploring?*

I decide to find out how she had experienced love and what had happened when she was younger. "What kind of loving did you get as a child?" I ask.

Her face reddens, as her eyes fill with tears. She hesitates. "I… think… I was loved…" she says, and immediately I have a clue. Her tone of voice indicates that she doesn't *really* believe what she has just said. If she only *thought* she had been loved, my guess is she hadn't fully *felt* loved.

She went on, "But then my parents split up when I was six, and I only saw my Daddy about once a month after that." The room feels heavy, leaden. I am weighed down as I imagine her disappointment at only seeing Daddy once a month. That would feel like forever to a six-year-old.

"Sounds like you really missed your father, seeing him only once a month?"

Tears fall down Sheila's face, though I can see her trying to hold back from crying. "It's okay, let the tears come… see if you can soften your jaw."

As she loosens her jaw, sobs come, her upper body curls over, and her body silently shakes.

"It's okay to make a noise," I encourage.

She lets go, and gives a stifled wail.

"There is no one around," I reassure her, "It really is okay to make a noise."

As a psychotherapist I often see people cry, but only once or twice have I seen anyone able to really cry for more than five or six minutes at a time. The crying usually comes in waves, so there may be another wave, and then another, but each wave only lasts a few minutes. Her sobs subside, and Sheila reaches for a tissue.

"I missed him so much," she says.

"I am going to make a suggestion, if you are up for it?"

She nods.

"Can we explore your relationship with your Daddy by using an imaginary father figure?" I wait, and when she gives a tiny nod I continue, "He would be an *Ideal* Father figure... He would be a completely new figure, not your real father, not even anyone you knew, but an imaginary figure who would have been married to your mother, and they would have stayed married." I wait, watching to see how she responds. Sheila, looks thoughtful, and I wonder if she is beginning to imagine this Ideal Father. Then her face changes, and she looks at me again. I take this as a sign that she is ready for me to continue. "He would have been the perfect partner for your mother, and an Ideal Father for you, and he would have been there for you when you were two, three, four, five years old, a six-year-old... a seven-year-old... and all the way through your childhood and adolescence. Could you imagine someone like that?"

She looks doubtful. "I can't imagine that."

I realise that I misread her a moment ago. "Which is harder to imagine, the Ideal Father for you, or the perfect partner for your mother?"

"Someone really being kind to me," she says wistfully.

"How might he have shown this kindness?" I ask.

"Well, I don't really know," she says. Then adds, "I guess he would have spent time with me."

"So, this Ideal Father, who is no part of your real father, would say to you," and here I gesture, indicating an (imaginary) figure standing beside her, and speaking to her. I continue, "He says, 'If *I* had been your *Ideal* Father when you were a child, I would have spent *time* with you."

She pauses, and gives a tiny nod.

I continue, gesturing to him again. "And then he says, 'And as your Ideal Father, I would have been kind to you.'"

Her face begins to soften. "There was a man up the street, Franny's father, and he was always very kind to me."

"Well," I say, "this Ideal Father would have had the *qualities* of Franny's father, but he would have lived with you and been *your Ideal* Father. The father who you needed when you were a child growing up." I pause briefly, and then ask, "Does that fit?"

"That would have been wonderful, if he had stayed while I was growing up."

I point, gesturing near her again, "He would say," and I lower my voice slightly, dramatising it to sound as if a man is in the room speaking to her, "'If I had been your Ideal Father when you were five years old, I would have loved your mother, and stayed married, and I would have been around while you were growing up.'"

She raises her eyebrows, slightly surprised. Then she smiles, breathes out and her body softens.

I can see that she is coming to accept this imaginary figure, and is already seeing him in her mind's eye. She says, "That would have been lovely. He'd have spent time with me every day."

I gesture again, to invoke her Ideal Father, picking up her words and using the 'Ideal Father voice'. "He says, 'If I had been your Ideal Father, I would have spent time with you every day.'"

"Oh my god! That would have been so wonderful. Yes, I can imagine that. That is what I needed. We would have played together. I could have rough-and-tumbled with him. I had to be so polite and careful with my real father. I didn't want to upset him in case he went away again. And anyway, we usually met in a Wimpy or a cafe, where we couldn't play."

Gesturing to where the Ideal Father stands, I say, "He would say to you, 'If I had been your Ideal Father when you were a child, we would have played rough-and-tumble games, and I would have been there every day, because I would have been living with you. You wouldn't have had to be careful with me. You could have relaxed, and known that I wouldn't have gone away. I would have been there, *with you*.'"

"Oh yes!" she exclaims. "That would have been marvellous. And I could have snuggled up with him."

"'If I had been your Ideal Father when you were a young child' he says, 'you could have snuggled up with me.'" I pause, then ask her, "How would it be if we enrolled the chair to represent the Ideal Father, then, as you lean against the arms of the chair, they could represent his arms, and you could feel his solid arms around you?"

"Let's try that," she responds.

"So the chair now represents your Ideal Father," I say, and gesture to the chair, "and he says, 'You can snuggle up with me.'"

She wriggles into the arms of her Ideal Father (the chair), and gives a deep sigh as if her whole being is letting go. Releasing. Then she begins to sob quietly.

At this point I bring in another symbolic figure to help acknowledge the feelings she's having, saying, "If there was someone here who was witnessing all this, then The Witness would say 'I see how much grief you feel as you remember what *didn't* happen, when you were a child.'"

She cries for a few minutes, and then quietens, letting out a big sigh.

"And the Witness would say, 'I see how much relief you feel as you imagine this new possibility with your Ideal Father. You could have snuggled up with him.'"

I pause for a moment while she processes this, and then I continue, slipping into teaching mode for a moment. "That is a normal cycle. When you taste the new possibility of how it could have been, then you feel grief, as you remember how it really was. Then the new possibility comes in again, and you feel relief as you allow yourself to imagine experiencing exactly what you needed with the Ideal Father, who would have been there, every day, and played with you, and then snuggled up with you."

Sheila nods.

"What is happening in your body now?" I ask.

"My whole body is buzzing, I feel alive, there's a lot of energy moving up and down. It feels great."

I gesture again, to where the Ideal Father is standing, "He says, 'With me you could have felt *this* alive and you would have grown up with *this much energy.*'"

She smiles, and sighs with relief, settling even deeper into the arms of her Ideal Father (the chair).

The repetition of the Ideal Father may feel a bit arduous as it is read from the page, but in the session it serves several functions. The reiteration reinforces the scene in her imagination, helping her experience new and different aspects of the childhood she wanted, and deserved to have. More importantly it helps Sheila to allow some separation from the words that come from me as the therapist, making them come from the mouth of the Ideal Father. This means that I don't become the primary means of healing; the Ideal Figure does the healing, and I merely facilitate the process.

I notice that Sheila is looking into the middle distance in such a way that I know she is remembering something. "What are you seeing?"

"Once Dad left, I never saw him and Mum together again."

"What was your Mother like?"

"She was under a lot of pressure as a single mum, so she was stressed, and I think she found her life really hard."

"Let's do a step?" I suggest. She nods, and looks willing.

"How about bringing in an Ideal Mother, who wouldn't be stressed, but would have been calm and relaxed, and life would have felt easy for her?"

"Okay," Sheila responds, sounding unsure yet intrigued.

"Where would you place her if we brought her into the room?"

"Over there," Sheila points to the corner of the room.

This surprises me, as I expected her to place her near her Ideal Father. It makes me wonder if she is recreating her childhood history, with parents who were not close. I double check where she imagines her Ideal Father, remembering that we had enrolled the chair to represent him, "And where is your Ideal Father?"

"Right here," she pats the arm of the chair.

"I have a suggestion. How about we have the two of them close together, so you know they are in a loving relationship?"

Sheila looks at me with surprise, as if this was a new thought. I think the idea of them being together was so alien that she hadn't been able to imagine it.

"Yeh... Yes! She could be here." Now she looks excited, and she points next to the Ideal Father.

"What would you like to hear from her, or from them?" I ask.

She says, "We would *always* stay together, and we would be loving and affectionate with one another."

"So they say," and I gesture with both my hands to help her envisage them together as a couple, "'If we had been your Ideal Parents when you were a child, you would have grown up with both of us, and we would have *always* stayed together, and you would have seen how loving and affectionate we were with one another. Every day.'"

"Gosh, how amazing."

And so the session continues, with me finding out from Sheila what she imagines would have happened in a really happy childhood, some of which she had never considered before. Then, using the Ideal Parents, who would have been her primary source of loving nurture, I help her to create the conditions for her own happiness, in a way that is completely believable to her, so that she will, quite literally, feel it in her body.

She is getting pleasure from imagining her Ideal Parents being a close couple. Soon we reach a crucial moment in the session. She says she wants her Ideal Mother to be loved unconditionally by the Ideal Father. I think, *Good. Here is my opportunity to explore this with her, and help her to think it through.* I point out that it needs to go both ways. If her Ideal Father was going to love her Ideal Mother unconditionally, then her Ideal Mother would need to love him unconditionally too. She nods. Then I ask about her real parents, and find out that there was a series of affairs, and that her real father was a heavy drinker.

I ask Sheila, "At what point would it be acceptable for one partner to leave the other person. Do you have to stay in a bad relationship forever? However badly you are treated?"

She replies, sounding very certain: "If there was more than one affair, regular drunkenness, or violence, then that would be enough of a reason to leave."

I pause, letting her words hang in the air, and then I challenge her, mindfully keeping my voice tone quiet and gentle.

"So that means that the love would not be *completely unconditional?*"

This begins a discussion about love in an adult relationship. I put a question to her: "I know most of us yearn for unconditional love, but how realistic is it to imagine that we will actually have unconditional love for, and from, our partner?"

She doesn't respond.

I go on, "It is easier to love unconditionally when things are going well. But most of us don't even manage that. Generally,

118

people want to change their partner a little bit! But if you do love unconditionally, what happens if you find out your partner has lied, cheated, or spent all your money? Very few will continue to feel completely unconditional love!"

She gives an ambivalent shrug.

"For a parent with a child it is different. That love should indeed be unconditional. Whatever the child does, even if they were to commit a horrible crime, the two people who should always be there for that child are his or her parents, not necessarily condoning the behaviour, but always there for them. So unconditional love comes from parents..."

Sheila looks doubtful.

"...or should come from the parents!" I continue. "However, in an adult partnership I take a more realistic view." I slow down a bit now, to give her time to consider what I am saying. "Most of us don't know how to love unconditionally. It's a nice idea, but an unrealistic, romantic expectation. Most who think they offer unconditional love are actually in an enmeshed and fused relationship." I pause.

"Let's think about this. What happens if you end up in an abusive relationship? No one should have to be a martyr, or tolerate violence or offensive behaviour. As I see it, we definitely have the *right* to leave a relationship, under certain circumstances. Actually, I guess you are doing that with the men that you meet – if they don't love you 'well enough' you leave them. You are not offering unconditional love, even though you seem to expect it from them!"

I pause and smile. "For clarity, I am certainly *not* advocating that we give up at the first sign of trouble. On the contrary, it is usually worth working through the difficult times and, personally, I would expect to stay in an established relationship that wasn't going well, for at least six months and maybe over a year, to see if we could improve it. Many people who leave a partnership go on to recreate very similar circumstances in their next relationship!

None of us are perfect, and almost all couples will hit challenging times. But I am talking here about our *expectation*, about the *fantasy* of unconditional love.

"It is only when each person has the genuine *right* to leave, that staying becomes a choice. There is a delicious sweetness in knowing that my husband is choosing to be with me. It is infinitely preferable to him staying *out of guilt*, or just because he promised me twenty years ago. Yes, it makes me more vulnerable. I have given him the right to walk away if he wants to. But not in a snap decision after one row – only after considered reflection over many months. And we've agreed that if it comes to that, we'll be talking a lot. He would discuss his concerns with me first." My voice softens. "To know I am chosen is lovely. And I love the fact that I am choosing to be with him too."

Sheila responds, "You've given me a lot to think about. I need to spend some time with that, but let's say you're right for a moment. What should actually have come from my parents? Because it is definitely true that some things were lacking."

We talk together for a while, getting clearer about what she needed as a child. Once we have established her requirements, we bring in the Ideal Parents again. Her Ideal Father starts by telling her how much he loved her as a child, whatever she did. She did not have to be clever or good, she didn't have to 'earn' his love. It was freely given, and he loved her just as she was. She realises, and tells me that this is the first time in her life that she has experienced unconditional love.

Sheila decides that her *Ideal* Parents would have had a healthy, balanced and mature relationship with each other, loving and committed from before she was born, and that it would have lasted until they died, and they would both have lived long, contented lives.

The final stage is to help her to store this experience, placing these Ideal Parents into the correct part of her brain, the part connected with her long-term memory.[1] I begin, "Let yourself really feel in your body what it would be like to have Ideal Parents who had an equal and loving relationship, where they each took care to be honest, faithful, loving and kind."

"Mmmm." Her face is serene, almost blissful. Her body is relaxed, and the room feels peaceful and gentle.

"When would you have needed all that?" I ask.

"When I was ten," she says, with no hesitation.

"Not younger?" I check, surprised.

"Well, I guess, so... Yes... Yes. Maybe when I was five... four or five."

"So they say," I gesture with both hands to the Ideal Parents, "If we had been your Ideal Parents when you were four or five years old, you would have seen us together, committed to one another, being loving with each other. You would have seen that as you grew up – when you were six, seven, ten... a teenager... a young woman... and as you grew into full adulthood."

"Yes," she murmurs.

I pause, then say, "So let yourself take *this* feeling in your body, and put it back into your history, as if planting the feeling, like a photograph in the timeline of your personal history. Starting from when you were four-years-old, you would have experienced this feeling, back then, with this Ideal Father, and this Ideal Mother, who really loved one another, and loved you."

"Gosh! If I had had this when I was that little child, my whole life would be different!"

"Yes, that's right..." There is such tenderness in the room, that I find myself softening my voice to match its quality. "Let yourself imagine, as you leave here today, carrying this feeling with you, imagine how tomorrow and the next day will feel different, now that you've had this history, with this Ideal Father who would have loved you unconditionally, and this Ideal Mother who would have been calm and restful." To keep

121

it balanced I say, "She would have loved you unconditionally too," although I think to myself, *She really needs to hear that unconditional love part from her Ideal Father.*

She nods, and looks up at me. I see that she feels accepted and loved for who she is. Not by me, but by her Ideal Parents. I know from my years of working with this method that the feelings she has just experienced will become embedded. She will internalise these Ideal Parents, and keep these feelings deep inside her, and be able to access them whenever the need arises. In future sessions I will help her to build on this.

Sheila came into the session with the hunger of a child, longing to be loved unconditionally by a partner, an up-until-now bottomless hunger. She has now been fed and nourished by the love of her Ideal Parents, in a way that will stay with her. I hope that this will make a huge difference in her next sexual relationship.

Sheila: Ten Months Later

Two halves may make a whole in mathematics. But relationships work best with two wholes.

T he first session had a profound impact on Sheila. At our next meeting she reported that she had begun to develop a sense of quiet confidence, and felt as if she had more solidity. "I didn't know I was lacking it, and it is subtle but profound. Something changed, and I feel as if I will never go back to being as I was. I feel fuller on the inside and there isn't a gaping hole anymore. I feel more sure of myself in the world. I still want a relationship, but I don't have the desperate feeling that I had, and if it doesn't happen...well I will live with that and be okay. Now I think that if I do find a relationship, it will be to enhance my life."

Sheila attended one-to-one therapy for four sessions. Between sessions, she thought about the man she was looking for, and created a collage, using pictures from magazines, of his character, qualities and values. "I want a man who is creative and interesting, so he has to be open-minded and curious about the world. However, I also want safety, so I don't want him going off to climb any mountains!" She laughed. She was honing and clarifying what she hoped for in a partner.

She comes to see me for our last one-to-one session. She tells me that she is quietly proud of her creation, and has hung it in her kitchen, where she can regularly see it, as a reminder of the kind of person she is looking for. We talk about the strengths and assets that she brings to a relationship, and explore her fears – the things that might be stopping her from moving forward. We look at lessons to be learned from previous relationships. She has become increasingly clear that she only wants someone who is going to really add to her life and her situation, and she decides that she will be more discriminating about who she chooses. "In the past, if *they* liked *me* that was enough! I didn't really stop to wonder if I really liked them too," she admits. "I think I was so grateful for the offer of a date, that I went out with anyone. But then, a few weeks in, they would often let me down, or disappoint me. Usually, I would want more from them than they wanted to give; I wanted them to text me more, or to telephone me. If they didn't do that I would complain. We might have a tiff. Generally, they would leave the relationship after around four or five weeks. Very occasionally I would be the one to end it, if I could see it wasn't going anywhere."

Realising that her childhood had played a big part in her neediness, and having found the Pesso Boyden System Psychomotor (PBSP) one-to-one work helpful, Sheila decided to join one of my closed PBSP personal development groups. The group meets for eight days over ten months. There are fourteen people in the group, men and women aged from their twenties to their seventies. Sheila commits to three structures.

A structure is a single client session. In this, the client externalises the inner landscapes of their heart and mind. This involves bringing the action out into the room, literally, with real life people taking roles and characters. These include the inner voices and figures that can, unbeknownst to us, govern our lives. At this point, memories often start to flood in.

The therapist and client together note the deficits, where the client didn't get what they needed as a child. They also log areas of trauma and intrusion, which could include cruel words, shouting, physical violence or sexual abuse. Then, using group members to role play Ideal Figures, they co-create a symbolic, alternative history. This is a 'new memory' that fits the client better. The client's perspective on life can shift. They often respond to life differently in the present, and may develop a greater sense of possibility in their future.

In a one-to-one PBSP session, the figures are created in the imagination, or using a blanket, pillow or chair to represent the Ideal Figures (as you saw with Sheila in the previous section). When PBSP is offered in a group context the client has the opportunity to use real people, the group members, to role play these Ideal Figures. This seems to reach and heal where talking therapy cannot.

As very small children, most of our communication and interaction is essentially physical. In PBSP we are replacing those early, not-ideal, physical memories with new, exactly-fitting, physical memories. Not only that, but most memories from that age are non-verbal. This means that some information can *only* be accessed through the body. Hence the healing antidote must also be taken in via the body. I write in more detail in Chapter 5 about using PBSP in groups.

In the first structure in the group, Sheila tells us: "My mother, Clare, became pregnant at a party." She looks downcast. "She was 23, but she didn't want me, she didn't want a child at all. I remember thinking that it was rather callous of her to have told me. I was only young when she talked about it." Sheila's father, Paul, had agreed to stay with her mother, but it was clear that they did not have a good start to their relationship. They hardly knew each other. Although they didn't actually split up until Sheila was six, Paul was rarely around after the first year. Not only that, but Paul's parents, who were very religious, had been horrified at the pregnancy, and had cut themselves off from Clare and Paul. When Sheila was born, her maternal grandfather had already died, and her maternal grandmother was emotionally distant, and lived a long way away.

In the structure, Sheila thinks about what she would have needed in her past in order to have been happy now. She conjures up Ideal Parents who are an exact fit for her. She decides that they would have known each other for two years before deciding to get married, and they would have been married for a further year before they thought about having a child. She would have been the longed-for child. Recognising how unsupported her mother was, she goes a step further, and enrols two sets of Ideal Grandparents, adding them to the scene. These Ideal Grandparents would have been delighted by the marriage, excited when their first grandchild arrived, and involved and supportive as she grew up.

My strongest image from this structure is of Sheila (a woman then in her thirties), lying across her Ideal Mother in a semi-foetal position, as if she is in her Ideal Mother's pregnant belly. I also remember, later in the same session, Sheila gazing up into her Ideal Mother's eyes, looking for all the world like a six-month-old baby. I recall her Ideal Mother looking back with such love and adoration that the whole room was touched. Her Ideal Father was sitting behind her Ideal Mother, with his hand reaching round onto Sheila's shoulder, attentive and present for both his wife and his daughter. By the end of her first structure, early nurture had started to become believable to her, and she felt (maybe for the first time) full on an emotional level, fed and satisfied. That piece of the puzzle was filled, and the 'hole' in the fabric of that piece of her history had been darned up.

In the second structure, the part I remember most clearly is Sheila's surprise and joy as she imagines herself as a five-year-old, and then as a six and seven-year-old, seeing her Ideal Parents continue to be together and united. It amazes me how much happiness an adult woman feels as she watches – as if from the perspective of her child-self – two adults role-playing Ideal Parents who would have stayed together. The Ideal Parents have their arms around one another's waist, gazing at each other with love.

The look of astonishment and pleasure on Sheila's face is a delight to witness. She holds her hands up to her cheeks as she chuckles with joy. It is as if Sheila has been yearning for this for a very long time, and seeing them together feels like the completion and satisfaction of a long-held dream. Since children learn so much from watching their parents, including how to be in a relationship, it is absolutely vital for Sheila to see her Ideal Parents interacting as a couple. It provides useful data for her about her own peer relationships.

In the third structure we revisit the issue of parent and partner. She chooses three figures: her Real Father, an Ideal Father and a Dream Partner (we use the Dream Partner as a tool to clarify what we might realistically expect from a partner). Sheila had always wanted a partner to 'be there' for her. We are working on her yearning for unconditional love again, but this time at a deeper level. As we talk she realises, understanding this in a different way, that her *Ideal Father* is the one who should have been there for her always. If she had had that as a child, then she might not be so hungry for unconditional love from a partner as an adult. Her Ideal Mother would also have been there to nourish and give her unconditional love from the start. They would have helped her to develop a sense of belonging, so that she knew she was welcomed in the family, and had a place in the world. With this start, she would have grown up respecting herself, filled up with her parents' love.

At a certain point, her Ideal Father in the structure says, "If I had been your Ideal Father, I would always have been there for you." But Sheila looks sceptical, and I can see that she does not really trust these words.

I think to myself, *She needs to test him, only then will she really believe it.* I ask her, "How could you check that he really means it?"

After some time, she says, "Well, I was never able to be cross with my real father." As she says it, she sounds both wistful and accepting. "I was too afraid that I would see him even less if I got cross with him, that he would reject me." Her once-a-month meetings with him when she was a child were very precious times.

We create a situation that she feels will represent her expressing anger towards her Ideal Father. She starts by standing opposite him, with her hands in front of her, palms facing outwards. His hands meet hers, his palms on her palms. As she pushes, he meets her energy, offering physical resistance. He can feel her power. She doesn't want him to overpower her, just to 'meet' her powerful energy.

Recognising this, I ask the Ideal Father to say, "If I had been your Ideal Father I would not only have *met* your powerful energy, I would have welcomed it too." Sheila looks him in the eye, and smiles. The man who is playing the role of her Ideal Father has a twinkle in his eye as he smiles back. I sense she is ready to experience an antidote to her childhood fear of her real father, so I ask him to say, "And if I'd been your Ideal Father when you were a child, you could have been angry with me. You could have expressed *all* your anger, and I could have handled it." I check with her, "Is that okay?" Her Ideal Father looks more serious now, which seems fitting. The expression on her face lets me know that this new information is landing, and that she feels good hearing it. She starts to push against him more.

Responding to the determined look on her face as she begins to really push him, using all her force, I ask him to say, "I would have helped you to express your anger, but I wouldn't have let you hurt me, and I wouldn't have let you hurt yourself. And I wouldn't have stopped your anger. I could have handled it." As he says the words, he gives Sheila such a loving and kind look. He is offering an implicit acceptance of, and blessing for, her anger.

Sheila surprises herself by roaring with fury and rage, and pushing with all her might. It takes a man enrolled as her Ideal Father, supported by two other men in the group, enrolled as extensions to the Ideal Father, to meet her energy and make sure that she doesn't push her Ideal Father over! After she has roared, she sobs with grief and relief, and her Ideal Father holds her. A release like this often happens after deep anger work. Following the grief, Sheila tells us that she is feeling deep pleasure and joy.

After each of the three structures, as she understands more about the man she is seeking, she adds images to the collage that hangs in her kitchen.

In a later one-to-one session we take a more practical approach, and brainstorm strategies for Sheila to meet a man. We discuss everything from joining evening classes and using internet dating sites (we work through her reluctance and embarrassment at having to do this), to asking her friends to connect her to possible candidates. We discuss the different stages of a relationship, and what she might do when the power struggle phase begins. I do this because I am wanting to check that Sheila doesn't have an overly romantic notion of relationships. She decides that she wants a partner who would be willing to go with her to find help from a therapist if it is needed. I pass on a piece of advice that I myself was given many years ago, which applies to anyone in a new relationship: "Don't do anything in the first thirty days that you are not willing to carry on doing for the next thirty years!"

Last time I checked, Sheila was in a relationship that had lasted for five months. She was feeling excited and hopeful that this one might last.

Thoughts and Theory:
PBSP – The Structure of a Structure

The past, we can be sure, plays both major and minor.
We may not choose to notice, but it's always there.
William Ayot[2]

Pesso Boyden System Psychomotor (PBSP) doesn't treat people as sick or broken, but comes from the perspective that, "We are all," as my teacher, Al Pesso the co-founder (along with his wife Diane Boyden-Pesso)[3] would say, "in the endless act of becoming wholly and truly who we are." PBSP works with the soul and the ego, the mind and the body, to help us to be consciously connected to our true self. Through historical antidotes, which create new memories, hitherto unknown aspects of the soul can be welcomed and blessed. It can be used in one-to-one (or one-to-a-couple) therapy (Kim and Rakesh in Chapter 3, and Sheila in the first section of this chapter), or in a group (Sheila in section 2 of this chapter, and in fuller detail in Chapter 5 with Josh and Chloe). Each situation is worked out by the client, with the help of the therapist, to create a precise counter-shape to what actually happened in the past.

Creating the precise fit

I too have been a client of PBSP. I loved the experience of working with my therapist to create a precise fit, carefully tailored to satisfy my original deficit or repair my initial trauma. Like slotting the final piece into place in a jigsaw, there is a feeling of bodily satisfaction that comes when the 'right words' – words that I have unknowingly longed to hear all my life – are not just said, but spoken with heartfelt meaning by the right person. It is as if an open sore that I have got used to living with for the last fifty years has suddenly healed, closed over, my whole body is soothed and I become quiet on the inside. I see this happening too, over and over, with clients in PBSP groups. Remember when Sheila said during her first structure, *"Gosh! If I had had this when I was that little child, my whole life would be different."*

Our history impacts our present and our future

Our history has a huge impact on our future, as well as our present. As William Faulkner[4] said, "Our past is never dead. It is not even past." This is because what happened in our past has such a profound influence on us. Sheila's history with her parents had left its mark. We saw how she felt abandoned by her father, and (unconsciously) expected to experience that abandonment again. She became suspicious of men, and needed extra reassurance that boyfriends were going to stay forever and love her unconditionally. Potential partners picked up on this neediness, found it stifling and stepped away. Another residue from her childhood was seeing her mum as a single mother. This left her with the (unconscious) expectation that women must manage on their own. She lacked the role models for a healthy, long-lasting couple relationship. Since her father was not around when she was a child, she didn't learn about how to relate to him, thereby losing a key opportunity to learn about men. She missed out on having her femininity blessed as a young-woman-approaching-adulthood, which is most effectively done by a father. Finally, she lacked essential nourishment, from both her mother (who didn't want a child) and her father (who had left). Sheila's description, that she'd had a gaping hole on the inside, indicated this. She was desperate to fill that hole – with something or someone!

The aim of PBSP is a life of pleasure, satisfaction, meaning and connectedness. To achieve this, we need to have lots of happy childhood memories, of our soul living its fullness in the world. When we have been nourished, nurtured and encouraged from the beginning, we can look forward to the future with hope and positive expectations. However, none of us have a blemish-free personal history, and the deficits in our childhood affect our behaviours, and create patterns that shape our expectations about the future and what it might hold.

The reason that most of us, as adults, have emotionally-fused relationships is due to our childhoods. We did *not* have our basic needs adequately met as children. This leaves us trying to get these needs met in our adult relationships. "We call that a marriage," Al Pesso jokes.[5]

Creating new memories

Al Pesso refers to PBSP as a 'new memory shop.'[6] The client is offered a fresh, positive, symbolic memory to offset the effect of any deficits or traumas in their actual history. Like sewing up a hole in the fabric of the client's history, we repair a 'rip' or a 'gap' where their needs were not met as a child. Then we link this 'new history' to the client's sense of themselves as a young child. This creates a domino effect. Many pieces of their history recombine to form a new picture. For example, when Kim in Chapter 3 imagined having an Ideal Grandfather who would have been gentle, I remember him saying, "If I had had *that* man in my history, an Ideal Grandfather who had not been violent with my mother, then my mum would not have learned to lash out when she was upset. Then I would not have grown up feeling afraid of Mum's anger. As an adult, I wouldn't have become a people pleaser, walking away from confrontations. And that would have changed everything…

my whole life would have been different." This single change, to a non-violent grandfather, had helped Kim to imagine a 'new history'. This was an important aspect in creating the history that Kim deserved and needed in order to be happy, as opposed to the real history he'd experienced. In PBSP we call this the 'antidote', as it gives a powerful alternative to the real, childhood memories.

Externalising the inner landscape

We start a structure (a client session) by helping the client to externalise the landscape of their inner world. They talk about what is happening right now in their life. Think of Sheila talking about wanting to be accepted and loved. From the start of the session, the therapist tracks the client's process by using a caring and benign 'Witness' figure who sees, hears and acknowledges the client's current experience and tiny emotional shifts. Remember in Sheila's one-to-one session[7]: *"If there was someone here who was witnessing all this, then the Witness would say 'I see how much grief you feel as you remember what didn't happen, when you were a child.'"* Other figures are brought in to help the client notice their (sometimes erroneous) thoughts and core beliefs. This all supports the client, helping them to develop awareness of the structure and architecture of their current thinking. We call this process 'micro-tracking the client's present consciousness'. It often triggers spontaneous memories from childhood that help the client to reflect on the impact of their history. Remember Sheila saying, *"[My mother] didn't want me, she didn't want a child at all."*

Working together with the client, the therapist uses this historical information to co-create an antidote, reversing the 'negative' historical experiences and imagining how it 'could-have-been' in the past if there had been the most favourable circumstances. I invited Sheila: *"Imagine having Ideal Parents who would have known each other for two years before deciding* to get married, who would have been married for a further year before they thought about having a child. *You would have been the longed-for child.*" The new experience is built up layer on layer, creating each believable step so that the client can really enter into the experience and absorb the healing from these symbolic figures. This gives the client a real, and bodily felt, experience.

As the structure unfolds, the client tunes in to their deeper self. They start to know what they want to hear, and who they want to hear it from. The location, words and the tone of voice are all incredibly important, and it is the job of the therapist: to firstly, help the client identify which Ideal Figures are required, and then to ensure that they deliver what the client needs in the very precise way that they need it – we call this *shape* and *counter-shape*. The need of the client is a *shape*, and the Ideal figures provide a *counter-shape* – a satisfying fit. Think of a hungry baby who is puckering its mouth for food (*shape*), the nipple provides the perfect *counter-shape*, providing the milk which satisfies the need.

Put the new memory into the hypothetical past

Using our innate capacity to 'time travel', the therapist helps the client to place this experience with the Ideal Parents, as a 'new' hypothetical memory in the past. It is as if the client is working in stereoscopic vision: having both a literal, 'here and now' felt experience in the present, whilst simultaneously placing it back in time – 'as if' it had happened in the client's childhood. Sheila's Ideal Parents told her: *"If we had been your Ideal Parents when you were four and five years old, you would have seen us together, committed to one another, and being loving with each other."* She is seeing them together, in the 'here and now', *and* letting her four-year-old self imagine seeing them together back in time. Just as our 'real' memories affect us both consciously and unconsciously, so do these 'newly-created' memories.

What we see affects our body

Since PBSP is a body-based therapy, in a structure we want the client to have a whole-body, fully vivid experience that will impact them deeply (more about this in Chapter 5). The client imagines how life would have unfolded if they had grown up with the good feelings provided by this antidote experience. Research[8] shows that the brain is actually firing in different areas after a structure, as the neural wiring has changed. Some of us may think of our minds and bodies as independent systems. Yet everything that we see (and hear) causes a physical response – although the sensations may be subtle. Our bodies are responding both to images that we see with our real eye, and to those that we create in our mind's eye.[9] You may never have thought about this, but the unconscious doesn't know the difference between reality and fantasy.

Notice what happens if you take a moment to vividly imagine a litter of Labrador puppies playing in a field of poppies. Now make a clear picture of a crying, dirty and hungry young child that is living on the streets. You are likely to have a body reaction in response to the image you create, even though it is in your imagination, and is not real. You can go further, and enhance that image by making it a movie rather than a still picture, bringing in sounds, sensations, tastes, and smells. Go back to your picture of the puppies. See the vivid colours, feel the breeze, hear the birds and the yelps of the puppies as they play, and smell the country odours around you. Or picture the young child looking longingly at you with hungry eyes, asking you for food. Smell the pungent street smells, hear the child quietly crying and the background sounds. If you pay attention you will notice that the picture produces a reaction in your body. You saw the image in your mind's eye, then your body responded. You had a physical experience. Masturbation works in the same way, as we vividly imagine a scene and our body becomes sexually aroused!

In a structure, the same mechanism helps clients to create a believable image of an Ideal Figure who would really be there for them. They too experience the symbolic as real, just as you did with the picture you saw in your mind's eye. Because an Ideal Figure will be precisely formed to fit a childhood need, the image created can have a very strong impact.

Healing happens with the right kinship figure

The therapist's job is to help the client identify the correct Ideal Figures for the most satisfying fit, and to help the client work out at what age, or ages, the need was lacking. The deficit needs to be filled by the *correct kinship relationship, and at the right age*.[10] This means that if, like Sheila, the cause of fusion is a deficit of *nurture* from her real father, then her partner will *never* be able to fill that up. The boyfriends that Sheila had a relationship with probably said, "However much I give, it is never enough. Sheila is like a bottomless pit." Or they may have said, "Everyone gives Sheila masses of love, but she simply doesn't take it in." It is as if Sheila is in the middle of a banquet of the most delicious food, that she longs to take in, and yet she still starves.

Your *partner* can never give you *now*, what your *parents* should have given you *then*. For example, if your mother didn't support you as a child, then as an adult you may feel insecure, ungrounded and have poor balance. Your partner won't fill that need for support, his or her input simply won't 'stick'. If your father shamed you for being angry when you were young, then you might grow up afraid of your anger, becoming a people-pleaser. Alternatively if, like Kim in Chapter 3, your mother had unexpected outbursts of rage that frightened you, you may grow up afraid that *you* could overpower and hurt people, and also be afraid of your anger. In either case, your partner is never going to be able to heal that. He (or she) is not the right person to bless your anger, because (s)he is the *wrong* kinship relationship. Since (s)he is not the family-of-origin member who created the fear, (s)he cannot be the source of the healing. Nor can your therapist. Again, he (or she) is not the right kinship relationship to you.

Sheila told us that there were two key moments that changed everything for her. The first was the acceptance and nourishment she felt laying across her Ideal Mother, and eye-gazing. The second was when her Ideal Father, the right kinship relationship, gave her unconditional love as a child, even when she was angry with him. She tested his love by pushing as hard as she could against him, and he was strong and steady. He did not retaliate, or withdraw. It seemed that this proved to her that her Ideal Father loved her, all of her, including her angry self. This new information – that she was a lovable person – settled into her body, and the feeling lasted.

Healing at the right age

The age is important too. Remember, these issues can only be fully corrected by the correct kinship relationship, *and at the right age*. If your partner tries to heal the wound, they are only able to act in the here and now. Since the deficit happened when you were a child, then the healing needs to be put back into that time frame too. I helped Sheila to link her Ideal Father to her younger self: *"He would have been there for you when you were three, four, five years old, six years old."* That connects it to her memory of herself as a child, at the right age. Later I invited her to, *"Take this feeling in your body, and put it back into your history, as if planting the feeling, like a photograph in the timeline of your personal history. Starting from when you were four years old."* Again, I was helping her to put the healing experience into her long-term memory, and her body memory, linked to the correct time frame.

Input not output

In PBSP the focus is on input (taking in – through words, touch or what we see), rather than output (such as catharsis or other expression). The input, or the healing, happens when the client 'takes in' from the Ideal Figures who say or do whatever it is that the client needs. As they *give*, the client *receives*. This 'taking in' can begin to fill the client up and patch up any 'gaps'. In some other therapies the important thing is the output – the expression of anger or tears. This catharsis can be beneficial, and we would never stop it in a structure. It often happens, and provides a release of tension, and helps to integrate impulses that may never have been felt or expressed. But generally, catharsis doesn't produce lasting change. People can cry or be angry again and again and again, but the issue is still there. It is much more effective to acknowledge the energy *behind* the feeling of fear, anger etc. We then track back to the root of that energy, to see what antidote is wanted – what the client needs to 'take in' in order to correct this deficit. By reversing the details of what *actually* happened, and putting in its place the vision of what *should* have happened, using the symbolic Ideal Figures, the client feels a deep sense of satisfaction, the 'click of closure', a sense of, 'Yes, that is just right. That is exactly what I needed', and when clients go out into the world they notice the difference.

As a therapist I constantly see how our family history affects us all, for good or ill. So many therapies would have given Sheila better coping strategies for living with the hole that the nurture deficit had left, or struggling with her unexpressed anger. What I find so amazing, and rewarding, about working with PBSP is realising that these early deficits don't have to be tolerated or managed. They can actually be *repaired*. Clients can thrive rather than just survive.

Chapter 5

Chloe and Josh

We start off wanting to change others. Then we grow and realise it is wiser to change ourselves.

Chloe and Josh contacted me to ask about the Pesso Boyden personal development groups that I run. We had a three way Skype chat.

"A friend is in your Oxfordshire group," Josh told me, "and he was recommending the work to us. We like the way he talks about it, and the changes we have seen in him in the last year, so we want to come and give it a try ourselves."

Chloe told me, "Every year we do something together, to put something *into* our relationship. One year it was a weekend workshop on intimacy, another year we did a Grief Ritual together. Most years we find some kind of personal development work to do together. We see it as a part of our self-development, and also a way to ensure that our love for each other grows deeper, and doesn't become stale. It is important to both of us."

Josh continued: "We see ourselves together in forty years' time, and we both know that in order to stay together we need to keep working on our relationship. I was married to someone else, and I took our relationship for granted, and we split up. That was a shock to me. Chloe and I both value doing 'our work', and this year we want to see where Pesso Boyden takes us. We get on well most of the time, but I don't want to let little niggles build into resentments. We need to have a way to clear stuff as we are going along. We don't have any big problems in our relationship, but I want to make sure it stays that way."

Chloe interrupted, smiling, "We get irritated with each other sometimes, just like all couples I guess."

Josh added quickly, "But mostly we get on pretty well, so this is just because we want to keep doing our inner work, and enhance our relationship." I notice how insistent Josh is that they are doing alright at the moment.

I start to tell them about the group and the method. "The aim is to help you to be more fully authentic, more of who you truly are. We help you to identify emotional deficits or traumas from your childhood, and then create a new, believable memory of the past that you would have needed – rather than the past that you actually had. The new memory sits alongside the original memory, supplementing it. We do this using Ideal Figures. The other participants will *role play* those Ideal Figures for you, if you want that, or you can simply create the Ideal Figures in your imagination.

"You may be asked to play a role for other people. But don't worry, I will give you the words that you need to say, so it is not difficult. People get a lot out of playing the roles for each other, and learn a great deal from watching other people's structures (which is the name for a PBSP client session). Sometimes you'll find you are unexpectedly touched by something that happens. For example, an Ideal Father might say, 'I would have been there for you when you were eight... and I would have protected you, I wouldn't have let you be hurt. You would have been safe with me.' This might touch you if you had a history where you needed protection. You'll often find that someone else's issue is close to yours, and you get some vicarious healing during their structure."

They join one of my groups. When I meet Chloe in person for the first time, I am struck by her quiet elegance. Not a classical beauty perhaps, but her long dark hair shapes her oval face with its full lips. She has a slender figure, and what seems like an effortless sense of style. Josh is tall, blonde, and solid in an athletic way. He seems slightly remote, and cautious.

Each module is two days, and it is now the second module. Chloe and Josh have already seen eight structures. They had chosen not to have a structure before now. We start the day with everybody 'checking in', taking it in turns to tell the group how they are feeling, what is happening in their lives, and letting us know about the changes they have noticed since we last met.

It is Josh's turn to have a structure. I sit opposite him, still and silent, waiting for him to speak. All I know about him comes from what I have seen as he interacted with members of the group in the first module. He hasn't told us anything about his history, or about what he wants to work on today. My focus is to create a field of heightened awareness and sensitivity, a space where he can talk about anything. I assume that this particular 'now' will contain everything he has learnt from his life so far. Josh begins, "I am struggling with Chloe. We've been having an unexpectedly hard time in the last few months. I don't really know what is going on, but I feel *got at* a lot of the time. Chloe is criticising me. *All* the time."

I gesture with my hand, as if I am invoking another person, who will witness his state of mind and his emotions. "If there was a Witness here, the Witness would say, 'I see how confused and pained you feel as you remember feeling got at and criticised by Chloe.'"

Josh nods. "Yes. I do."

I say, "Let's put out a Placeholder for Chloe. A Placeholder..." I gesture to a pile of cushions, and a box containing stones, buttons, shells and other small objects, "is an object that represents *everything* to do with Chloe, like a filing cabinet of all the good things and all the challenging things about her."

Josh gets up and goes to the pile. He spends time sifting through, and chooses a four-inch square piece of rough cut slate. He turns to look at me, not sure what to do next.

I nod. "Place it somewhere in the room, wherever feels right to you."

He puts it just over two metres away, in front and to the left. Then he gazes at it for a long time. "She can be quite hard and has sharp edges. But I know there's a soft heart in there too."

I gesture to where I had previously indicated the (imaginary) Witness Figure is sitting, and said, "If there was a Witness here the Witness would say, 'I see how downhearted you feel that she can be quite hard and have sharp edges, *and* how touched you feel to know her soft heart.'" Then I remind him that this is a Placeholder, which encompasses *all* of Chloe's qualities.

Josh nods.

I think to myself, *Chloe is in the room, listening to this. I wonder, how is she feeling?* Then after a bit, another thought comes in, *This seems a big deal for Josh. I wonder if there is something from his history that is adding to his reaction to Chloe.*

After a long pause, Josh continues, hesitantly, and with frustration, "I get so fed up when she puts me down."

I gesture to where the (imaginary) Witness is. "The Witness says 'I see how pissed off you feel, when she puts you down.'"

"And tired. I've had this all my life, and I don't need it."

I gesture again, so it seems as if the Witness is affirming, "Exhausted!"

Josh looks very directly at me. It is as if he feels really seen. "Yes. I do feel exhausted. I had this in my childhood. My mother used to put me down. I could *never* do enough for her."

I think, *He has changed gear. He was talking about Chloe, and suddenly he is thinking about when he was younger.* I invite him to choose another object. "Let's have a Placeholder for your mother."

Josh chooses a small, grey rock with jagged edges, and places it on his right-hand side, just under two metres away.

I gesture so he knows it is the Witness speaking, "The Witness would say 'I see how utterly drained you feel, as you remember that you could *never* do enough for your mother.'" Then I point to the jagged rock, "So *that* is a Placeholder for your real mother."

Josh sighs wearily. "Yes, kind of depleted. I remember coming home with exam results. I had eight As and one B, and the only thing she said to me, in fact she kind of barked it at me, was 'What happened? Why did you get a B?'"

"Let's reverse that. Imagine an Ideal Mother... an Ideal Mother who would be no part of your real mother, but would be the mother that you needed back then..." and here I dramatise my voice, to indicate another person talking, and gesture to a place just behind him to show where this person is standing, "... and she would say... 'If *I* had been your Ideal Mother when you were a child, and if you had come home with just one B, I would have been *so delighted*.'"

"That's not really believable," Josh replies.

Bringing in the whole Ideal Mother concept was too much for him, I silently reprimand myself. *I should have used a 'bookmark' for her.* A 'bookmark' is the first whisper of the Ideal Mother, just an indication of her that can be expanded later in the session. It is a marker for her place in the structure, and is used to avoid the client rejecting the too-big-at-this-stage idea of the Ideal Mother. "That's okay. It doesn't have to be believable just yet."

"I'm remembering. I was a really good swimmer, yet I think Mum only came to watch me once. I used to have to get a lift to the competitions with my friend. His parents would always take him, and me. They knew how to celebrate and they would have cakes if he had done really well. *My* family barely asked me how I had done."

I gesture to where the Witness sits, "The Witness sees how sad you feel when you remember envying your friend, and how

145

desolate you feel when you remember that your family barely asked how you had done."

I pause for a moment, then I gesture to the place I had previously indicated for the Ideal Mother. "She says, 'If I had been your Ideal Mother, I would have taken you to all your swimming competitions, and loved watching you. I would have congratulated you, and celebrated with you just for making the effort, just like your friend's parents did.'"

Josh nods, sighing, and visibly relaxing, "That would be good."

Good, now he is taking it in, I think to myself.

I gesture, "The Witness sees how much of a relief it feels to imagine that possibility."

Josh sounds surprised, as if he hadn't noticed the relief until the Witness pointed it out. "Yes, it does, I feel calmer!"

"Given that we have a group of people here, how would it be if someone role-played that Ideal Mother for you?" I ask.

"I am not sure that I am ready for that yet," Josh responds.

Too soon again, I think. I always encourage the client to guide the process and let us know what does or does not fit for them. I am talking here to the client's 'pilot' – the part of them that oversees everything and makes all the decisions. I reassure myself, *It's good though, that he can say no to me, and isn't just being a compliant client.* "Okay. Let me know if you want that later on."

"Okay. It's been interesting thinking about this, because I am realising just how unsupportive and critical my real Mum was. When I was doing my maths homework, which I had to do in the kitchen because I didn't have a table in my bedroom, she would come and look over my shoulder and say, 'Don't be so stupid. That isn't the right answer!' She didn't let me do things. She would take over and do it for me. I remember trying to build a model aeroplane, and she finished it off. She didn't let *me* do it. She thought I couldn't do it," he pauses, thinking. "She said 'No' a lot of the time."

I point to where the Ideal Mother was standing, and being careful to use a gentle voice, to counteract his real mother's criticism, I say, "Your Ideal Mother would have said, 'If I had been your Ideal Mother when you were a child, I would have encouraged you, not criticised you. And I would have found a very gentle way to show you how to do things. I would have let you experiment with doing things your way, and let you do things on your own. I wouldn't have taken over with your model aeroplane, or anything else. And... I would have said 'yes' to you more often than I said 'no.'"

Josh visibly eases as he sighs and sits back in the chair. "That feels really good. Yes, I can imagine that. God, I needed that! Instead of the constant undermining criticism that came from Mum."

I can tell from his reactions that he is now beginning to believe the words of the Ideal Mother, and they fit him. He is feeling relief. This is how it should have been for him when he was a child.

I ask, "Can I speculate with you for a moment?" Josh nods, agreeing, and I continue, looking down at the objects on the floor: "I'm looking at these Placeholders, the one for Chloe and the one for your real mum, and I wonder if sometimes, when you see Chloe, it is as if you are *experiencing* her as critical, just like your mother was."

He pauses, "Yes, that might be true."

I wait a moment, to let him absorb this idea. When he looks up, indicating he is ready, I say, "When that happens, we call it the Principle. In this case it would be the Principle-of-Your-Mother, which you see in Chloe." I check to see that Josh is with me, and he seems accepting of this. "Let's use a tiny bit of tissue to represent the Principle-of-Your-Mother; it is *her* criticism that you have been seeing, and let's place that Principle onto the Placeholder for Chloe. That's what is happening at the moment. I think you are reacting to Chloe more strongly because of your history with your mother." I wait to see him take this in. "If this has been getting

147

in the way of your relationship with Chloe, it would be good to tidy that up..." I pause, and then continue, "Before the end of the session we will need to move that Principle-of-Your-Mother *off* Chloe, and move it back to where it belongs, which is with your real mother. That might shift how you feel about Chloe. Does that fit? That your history with your mum has, in some ways, been contaminating your current relationship with Chloe?"

Josh nods, accepting, as he tears off a tiny piece of tissue. He rolls it between his fingers, and then looks at me.

"Place it on top of the Placeholder for Chloe, because that represents what is happening in your perception at the moment."

He places the tissue carefully on top of the piece of slate acting as a Placeholder for Chloe, and then checks, "So I am reacting to Chloe more strongly, because I had a mother who criticised me?"

"Yes, I think so, what do you think?"

He nods. I point to the piece of tissue. "So that represents the Principle-of-Your-Real-Mother."

"Okay, I get that. I think that is right. But I still have the history of my mum putting me down."

"So we sort that out with the Ideal Mother, who says," and I gesture, "'If I had been your Ideal Mother, I would *never* have put you down.'" I pause so he can take this in, and then ask, "What age did you need to hear that?"

Josh responds quite quickly, "From when I was two years old."

I indicate to the Ideal Mother. "She says, 'If I had been your Ideal Mother, no part of your real mother, but your *Ideal* Mother, I would *not* have criticised you when you were two years old. All the way through, as you grew up, I wouldn't have put you down.'" I wait for this to land. "What would she have done instead?"

Josh suddenly looks excited, and I can see he is already imagining this in his mind's eye. "She would have praised me." Then he says, "I think I am ready for a person now."

"Good. Who would you pick?" I look round the group, indicating that he can choose whoever he wants from the members of the group. Some look expectantly at him, some look down.

He turns to Sharon. "Would you do that?"

Sharon smiles, "Yes, I'd love to."

I say to Sharon, "Can you say to Josh, 'I will take on the role of your Ideal Mother'?"

Sharon looks at Josh and says, "I will take on the role of your Ideal Mother." She then waits for the next instruction.

I turn to Josh, "Where do you want to place her?"

He gestures to his right, close to him, "Right here, sitting."

I ask another group member to bring over a bar chair, which is twenty centimetres higher than the bucket chair that Josh is sitting in, and place it beside him. This means that when the Ideal Mother sits down, there is an appropriate parent-child height differential, which makes the new memory more believable. The Ideal Mother takes her place.

"What would you like to hear from her?" I ask.

"That she wouldn't have criticised me. Maybe she would sometimes praise me," he says.

I turn to the Ideal Mother and say, "Say to him..." and then I change my voice to a loving, warm tone, hoping she will copy both the words and the timbre, "'If I had been your Ideal Mother when you were a child, I wouldn't have criticised you. *I* would have *praised* you.'"

This is repeated to Josh by his Ideal Mother.

"But then I wouldn't have learnt to try so hard," Josh says.

It is interesting to see Josh wanting to take the words in, but also struggling. As the therapist here I need to help him find the right configuration, one that really fits him, so that he will be able to let it in. It's like finding that perfectly-shaped piece for the middle of the jigsaw puzzle.

I say, "The current research shows that the best parents praise their children for making an effort, rather than for the results that they actually produce."

Josh responds, "I like that. Yes, that would be good, that would work."

I speak again to the Ideal Mother, and indicate that she should repeat these words to Josh. "If I had been your Ideal Mother, when you were two years old, I would have praised you every time I saw you making an effort, or having a go. As you grew up, when you had a go at climbing on a slide, or making an aeroplane, I would have let *you* do that. I wouldn't have interfered."

The session continues. I notice he is leaning towards his Ideal Mother. This suggests that he might be yearning for some physical contact, so I ask him, "How could you embody this, your experience of this Ideal Mother who would have praised you?"

At first, Josh asks her to put her hand onto his shoulder. Then, suddenly, he looks astonished. "I don't *ever* remember being held by my real mother," he says. A few moments later he asks the Ideal Mother to move in closer, and hold him. She turns, and wraps both arms around him, drawing him to her, with one hand gently holding his head to her chest. He snuggles right into her, holding her tight and starts to sob.

Pointing to the Witness Figure, I say, "The Witness sees how heartbroken you feel that you don't have memories of being held like this by your real mother... is that right?"

Josh nods. After a while he quietens, and then lets out a huge sigh. It feels like years of tension and holding are released. He blows his nose.

I continue, indicating it is still the Witness Figure who speaks, "And how much relief you feel to imagine this possibility... of having been held by your Ideal Mother when you were a child."

Josh carries on, letting us know what he wanted to hear, that his Ideal Mother would have been loving, that they would have had lots of hugs, and that he could have cuddled up on the sofa with her to watch television when he was a child. In the session, he cuddles up to her for ten or twelve minutes, much of it in silence. Then he begins to shift position, and looks up at me. He reaches out to stroke his Ideal Mother's arm. "God! That felt marvellous."

His behaviour indicates that this part of the work has been done, and he is feeling satisfied and ready to move on. I am aware that we have one more piece to do before we complete the session, which is to move the Principle-of-His-Mother off (the Placeholder for) Chloe, and put it back where it belongs, on (the Placeholder for) his real Mother. I talk this through with him, and ask him how he wants to do this. I let him know that I could do it, a group member could be enrolled to do it, or he could move it. He decides to do it himself.

"In that case, I would ask that you take a moment, because this is an important symbolic move you will be making. Do it like a ritual ceremony, take it seriously."

Josh bends down, pauses, and then plucks the tissue off the Placeholder for Chloe.

I say, solemnly, "You are taking the Principle-of-Your-Mother off Chloe, as it doesn't belong there."

Josh moves over and slowly places the tissue onto the Placeholder for his real mother.

I continue, "And putting it back where it belongs, which is with your real mother."

I wait until I can see he has processed this. "What is happening in your body, having done that?"

"Well, it is really interesting," he says, sounding surprised. "I feel lighter. My body feels easier."

I gesture to the Placeholder for Chloe. "And when you look at Chloe what do you see now?"

Josh responds, still taken aback. "She looks clearer. Yes, she looks different. Better."

Then I ask, gesturing, "And if you look at the real Chloe over there, what do you see?"

Josh turns, looks, and a broad smile breaks out on his face. "I just feel full of love for her, and I see her warm loving heart."

Chloe is smiling back at him – in fact the look that passes between them has such a depth of love that I find myself feeling very moved.

I say "The Witness sees how tender you feel when you look at Chloe, and how full of love, and satisfied.'"

Josh nods. He looks at me, and smiles. "Yes."

"Just for clarity," I say, "it isn't that Chloe won't ever criticise you in future. She is your partner! I am sure that she will!" The group chuckles in recognition. Then I soften my voice indicating that this is an important distinction, "But when she criticises you in future, you won't hear your Mum's voice in the background, consciously or unconsciously, putting you down. What we have done today is to take the *historical load* off, so that Chloe can say what she wants, and you will just hear it as Chloe speaking. In fact, you will hear it more easily, because it won't tap into your wounded place. You're less likely to overreact. It won't hurt you as it might have before. And more than that, you won't be imagining criticism when it isn't there. We have cleaned things up so you just have a here-and-now response, not a response that is loaded due to your history around criticism. Does that make sense?"

"Uh huh." Josh grins, and again looks lovingly at Chloe. I sense he is imagining this new aspect to their relationship.

The last stage is to de-role, firstly the Placeholder for his real Mother and the Principle, then the Placeholder for Chloe, then the Witness Figure in the air. Then, finally the Ideal Mother. I look at her. "Can you say to Josh 'I am no longer role playing your Ideal Mother, I am Sharon?'"

Sharon does this, and moves back to her original seat. I also move my chair, which had been opposite Josh, and take a place in the circle. Then, starting with Chloe (because she is his partner), I offer the group a few minutes to share their reactions about what has happened. I invite them to speak about anything that resonates with their own issues, has touched them, or to let us know what it has been like to play a role. I ask them to direct their words to me, and to look at me as they speak, so that Josh can hear what they say, but doesn't have to respond in any way.

Chloe says, "Gosh. I had no idea it would be so moving to be here when Josh did his structure. Seeing him upset was really difficult, and I wanted to give him a hug. Boy, was I relieved when you moved that principle off me!" The group chuckle sympathetically at the surge of energy and the relief that she is feeling.

I notice, out of the corner of my eye, that Josh is nodding as she says this, but as requested, the group is looking at me rather than at him. Sharon says, "It is so moving to play the role of an Ideal Mother. It was *so* lovely to be able to really spend time with 'my son', and I really felt that I would have been a mother who could have let my child grow up with my support but without my interference. It was as if I accessed that part of myself in order to play the role, and I feel I have benefitted from that too. It was a privilege. I learnt something new about mothering today. Thank you."

Chloe and Josh: Three Months Later

The idea of being okay is one thing,
but the experience of being okay – wow! That is a whole 'nother thing!
A client, talking about their PBSP work

Now it is Chloe's turn to have a structure in the group. She sits, waiting for the group to settle, and again I notice her delicacy. I notice a deep sadness in her eyes. I sit, waiting with her. In Pesso Boyden we start from where the client is, in the here and now. In the early phase of a structure I am quiet, reflecting back to the client in different ways, through the Witness Figure, and externalising their inner Voices, but not intruding on their process with my own thoughts. Chloe looks around the room one more time. We are meeting in a large lounge in someone's home. There are pictures of landscapes on the wall, and shelves with books and ornaments on. There are twelve people in the group, sitting on a variety of kitchen chairs, armchairs and sofas, in a circle.

I am sitting opposite Chloe. She starts to speak softly: "I don't ever feel good enough, and it stops me from being who I really am." It is so quiet, it is as if she is pulling me in to hear her words, rather than speaking them out into the room. She gives an impression of vulnerability. It is as though one could fall into her eyes. She does not meet my gaze, and it feels to me that there is a hollowness behind her eyes, an endless void.

I hold my hand up, to gesture – as if there is another person sitting next to me, who is talking, and I say, "If there was a Witness here, then the Witness would say, 'I see how open and defenceless you feel as you think about not feeling good enough, and how that stops you from being who you really are.'"

She nods. The session begins to unfold, and in less than ten minutes she is telling us that her uncle had sexually abused her when she was a child.

"When it was happening it was as if I wasn't there. I would zone out, escape, detach from everything that was happening. I would go off into a kind of a daydream state."

I say, gesturing to where the Witness sits, "The Witness sees how subdued you feel as you remember that pattern of zoning out and detaching from everything that was happening." This disassociation is quite common in people who have been abused. It is a coping strategy.

In situations where abuse has occurred, the person has been pushed into something that they did not want to do. As the facilitator, it is my job to ensure that nothing unexpected happens to Chloe, which is particularly important where there has been intrusion. I make a mental note to be very sure that I give Chloe control at every stage, and check every interaction with her, to establish that she is ready for each step, and that it fits her. Chloe and I will work together to find the best words for the role figures to say to her. I don't want the role figures to improvise – this is important in every PBSP structure, but especially with someone who has experienced abuse. During the structure, I will make suggestions, but I am the only person in the room that does that, and Chloe holds the right of veto throughout the process. With Chloe, maybe because she was really ready for her structure, or maybe because she had done other workshops and one-to-one therapy, the following phases all happened in one session. But quite often a similar sequence of healing will take place over two, three or even four structures.

"Just talking about it makes me feel afraid," she says. She is visibly anxious and distressed. "Although I've touched on this many times, I've never *really* talked about this in depth before."

The fact that it had been held in for so long, never fully expressed, makes the fear feel almost overwhelming. I ask, "Do you want to bring in someone to be with you while you experience those feelings? Someone from the group, who can help and support you as you contact those big feelings."

She enrols someone from the group, a woman, as a 'Contact Figure to be with you – in contact with you' and places her in a chair right next to her, so their arms are touching. Then I see her settle slightly, and it is as if having this person beside her gives her extra courage. She begins to describe the fear of being eight-years-old, and of knowing that her uncle, who had been babysitting, was coming upstairs.

"He is coming for me, and I know he will kiss me and put his tongue in my mouth," and as she speaks, her body has an automatic reaction, pulling back. She looks like she could vomit.

I gesture to where the Witness sits. "The Witness sees how utterly revolted and disgusted you feel as you remember your uncle coming upstairs. Is that right?"

I make a suggestion: "Let's bring in a Protection Figure who could have shielded and safeguarded you when you were a child." She agrees, but asks if she can have two. We enrol two people, and place them, standing, about one and a half metres in front of her, facing away from her, which is the classic place for a protection figure to stand.

I ask Chloe, "Would it be okay if the Protection Figures say to you, 'If we had been there back then, we would have known what was going on, and we would have stopped it. We would never have let your uncle babysit for you.'"

Chloe nods agreement.

I repeat the words, this time I am looking at the Protection Figures, indicating to them that they will say those exact words to Chloe. The Protection Figures then speak in unison, duplicating both the words and the tone of voice that I used, "If we had been there back then, we would have known what could happen, and we would have prevented it. We would never have let your uncle babysit for you."

"My shoulders are really aching," she says. My intuition tells me that now she has the protection in place, her body might be ready to work with the fear. When something starts to happen in the body, I look for the correct counter shape – the most fitting and satisfying response – to this movement.

I suggest that Chloe moves her shoulders to see what they want to do. She raises her shoulders and shortens her neck, as if she were a tortoise pulling a shell over her, so she could hide. I ask her if someone could enrol as a Resistance Figure who could provide some pressure, some resistance to her moving her shoulders up. This is not to stop her, but the extra effort she will have to put into raising her shoulders will make her more aware of the feelings behind this impulse. She agrees and chooses someone, who comes to stand behind her and gently pushes down on the top of her shoulders. It seems that this helps her to connect to her fear and experience her feelings, because suddenly she begins to scream. It is the kind of high-pitched scream you would hear from a terrified animal. The scream continues, and then her legs start to tremble. The scream subsides.

I am paying close attention, I was half expecting that her legs might start to quiver or shake. Al Pesso started his working life as a dancer, and is very attuned to how the body responds. He has taught me that this phenomenon frequently occurs in people who have been abused. He sees it as directly connected to a boundless openness and vulnerability[1] in the client. (I write more about this in the following theory section.)

I direct Chloe's attention to what is happening in her legs, and let her know that this sometimes happens in people who have been abused. I briefly teach her, letting her know that there is often an unconscious impulse to open the legs, but the more conscious part of her doesn't want to do that, and I suggest that may be causing the trembling. I offer some Limiting Figures to hold her legs together, to keep them completely closed. I explain the thinking behind this to Chloe: "There is a surprising thing that happens to a person when they are being abused, they may submit in order to appease the abuser. This is an inbuilt, primitive, survival response. When all else fails we open to the attacker, in a kind of, *'Here I am, take me, but don't kill me,'* way. You may have heard of this. In the context of a kidnapping it is called the Stockholm Syndrome.[2] It is a psychological phenomenon where the hostage develops positive, loving feelings for the captor, and opens to them, as a way to survive. What better thing can we offer than sex? It is a natural mechanism designed to keep us alive, and we see it in primates[3] too. The problem is that it can leave people who have been abused with too much openness and vulnerability. It is nothing perverse, it is just an innate impulse. The trembling in your legs is the body instinctively opening, whilst another part of you is trying to protect you by keeping you closed."

The aim of having the Limiting Figures is to help Chloe to stay with the energy that she had avoided in the past, by disassociating from, or suppressing, the feelings. Actually tuning in to what she has suppressed will help her to discover that her feelings are manageable. This will help her to own and integrate her vulnerability and openness. She chooses two women as Limiting Figures who sit on the floor and put their arms around her knees, holding them really tightly together. I tentatively offer some words, checking with Chloe if they fit her. She nods, so I direct the Limiting Figures to repeat to Chloe: "We'll help you to handle how scared and vulnerable you feel, and make sure you stay closed and unharmed."

At my suggestion she starts trying to open her legs. The Limiting Figures do their job well, and hold them tightly closed.

"Let yourself make some sound," I invite.

Chloe exerts her full force, trying to open her legs. She goes red with the effort, and suddenly screams, high-pitched, penetrating and haunting. It is a shocking sound, but I was expecting it. I look at the two women who are role playing the Limiting Figures to check if they are OK. Seeing their determination, I feel pleased and reassured that they will not let her open her legs even a tiny bit.

Then the screams change into sobs, she turns her body to clutch onto one of the Limiting Figures, who wraps her arms around her. With Chloe's permission I quickly expand her role from Limiting Figure to Ideal Mother. Then (prompted by me) she says, "If I had been your Ideal Mother when you were a child, I would have held you whilst you felt your fear. It would have been safe for you to feel your fear with me. I would have helped you handle all your feelings."

It is very moving to see her, curled into a foetal position, holding on to her Ideal Mother, sobbing. After a while, the quality of the sobs changes, and I sense she is moving into her anger. I give the words to the Ideal Mother (checking with Chloe that they sound fitting to her) and the Ideal Mother repeats to Chloe, "It would have been safe for you to experience your anger with me too."

"I feel so furious," says Chloe, sitting taller now, her voice a bit louder. "How dare he do that to me? He should be castrated for what he did!" There is a long pause. Then her energy suddenly collapses and she softens her voice, "But I shouldn't feel that... he was my uncle."

Her guilt is shutting down her anger. I explain that it is perfectly natural to feel the need for revenge, and that we can work with these feelings on a symbolic level. I ask the Ideal Mother to say, "If I had been there, as your Ideal Mother, when you were a child, I would have let you feel your murderous rage, but I wouldn't have let you literally hurt him, or yourself."

"My dad should have been there too," she says. She chooses and enrols a man to play her Ideal Father, and asks him to sit on the other side of her with his arm around her, making contact with both her and her Ideal Mother. She talks about how her real father had been an alcoholic. He used to get very angry, and no one else in the family dared to express anger. Somehow his anger trumped everyone else's.

The Ideal Father says, "If I had been your Ideal Father when you were a child, I would have been a calm and gentle man. I would have been sober, not an alcoholic. There would have been space for *your* anger, for you to be angry."

Then she is moving into another phase, suddenly talking about how much she misses the contact with her uncle, and how fond of him she had been as a young child. Now she avoids all contact with him.

In the structure we bring in someone to represent the Loved-Aspect-of-her-Uncle.[4] Chloe needs to be able to express her love and tenderness to this man: emotions that she has never been able to show, because of the historic abuse that had happened. This step needs to be handled delicately. By using a separate person in the role of the Loved-Aspect, this allows her to cleanly sort out and express these feelings without the fear that he will misinterpret and misuse her love. The (person representing the) Loved-Aspect never responds in a structure. The only response will come from her Ideal Uncle. We enrol two more people to represent her Ideal Aunt and her Ideal Uncle. Her Ideal Uncle says (prompted by me, and with Chloe's permission), "If I had been your Ideal Uncle when you were a child, you could have expressed your sensuous self with me, and I would have had really clear, strong, appropriate boundaries. I would *never* have acted sexually towards you." Then he turns to look at the Ideal Aunt, "I would have been satisfied by my wife in every way, including sexually." Then looking at Chloe, "You would have been *entirely safe* with me."

Chloe has tears in her eyes and breathes huge sighs of relief as her body deeply relaxes. "That is such a relief. That feels soooo good," she says, with immense gratitude in her voice. She is relaxing and snuggling into her Ideal Mother as she speaks. I notice many of the group are smiling, and two have a tear gently rolling down their cheeks, touched, as they witness her deep peace and contentedness.

In the sharing I invite Josh as her partner, to speak first. "I knew about the sexual abuse, but we haven't really talked about it, and I didn't know many of the details. I didn't even know who it was. Gosh, that was so moving. There was something beautiful about it too, to see her going where she needed to go. It is a relief that she has opened up about it, as it was the one 'no go' area that I felt we had. I am grateful to the group. I could feel everyone was there supporting and witnessing Chloe – thank you. I am so proud of her, she was so brave. I understand now why she was slow to trust me at the start. I can be cautious around people too, though nothing like that ever happened to me. But I feel proud of her, and moved and…" He momentarily pauses, too choked to continue. "I just really love her."

Other members of the group, in the sharing, speak of the admiration and compassion they feel, and about how brave she was, and how her courage has touched them. One describes how full of anger she feels that this had happened to Chloe, and one of the men quietly and falteringly says: "I too was abused." I am always struck when someone reveals something of this nature. It brings the group together, as we are all touched by our common humanity.

Later Chloe tells us, "I felt we got straight to the heart of the situation. I feel more robust somehow." The session has been an important turning point for her. Over the next two modules I notice simple changes. Her voice seems louder, she talks for longer in the group, and stops apologising for what she is saying. It is as if she has earned the right to take her time and her space. She and Josh seem solid, and I notice how at the end of each of the 'group days' they are even more affectionate with each other, and more appreciative of what they have together.

Thoughts and Theory: PBSP in a Group
Touch, Trauma and Vulnerability

We are made to be able to be happy in an imperfect world that is endlessly unfolding.
Al Pesso[5]

BSP was originally designed to be used in groups. The groups that form may last for just one day, a weekend, a four-day residential, or for eight days over a year. There are many benefits to working in a group, but an important one is that the client can choose real people to role play their Ideal Figures. Maybe it is because I am not good at imagining, but when I am the client having a structure, I find nothing more powerful than having a real person role playing my Ideal Mother, looking at me with loving eyes and saying, "If I had been your Ideal Mother when you were seven years old, you would have felt my loving warmth and complete acceptance of you."

Some benefits of PBSP in a group

Being in a group gives everyone the opportunity to play roles for other people. This can, in itself, bring great insights and healing. A welcome change for some, when role-playing an Ideal Mother or an Ideal Father, is that they no longer feel like the 'needy client'.

Watching other group members' structures is a good way to develop awareness of our own issues. For example, if you find tears rolling down your face every time an Ideal Father stands up for his child, that is a clue that there may be an inner longing to experience that for yourself. Our reactions to seeing other people's work give us information about issues that may have been lurking, undiscovered, in our own history. Furthermore, recognising that everyone is dealing with their issues normalises our problems, and group members come to recognise that they are not the only one facing challenges.

The end of a structure, the antidote phase, almost always brings with it a positive shift of energy. It is often very beautiful, and everyone in the room benefits from it. Whether it is due to our mirror neurones[6] (scientists have discovered that when we see something happen to someone else, the same part of our own brain starts to fire too), allowing us to really feel what is going on for someone else, or our ability to 'hitchhike' on someone else's issues when they are similar to ours, or merely the pleasure of watching someone else's healing happen, it is profoundly therapeutic for the whole group.

In PBSP the client can be safely held and touched

Having real people available in the group allows the client to have an even more physical experience of the antidote (the precisely fitting 'alternative history'), than if they are working one-to-one. I was a 'talking therapist' for ten years before I came across PBSP. It has been very exciting to find a safe and boundaried way of working with the body, enabling the client to get the physical contact and touch that they need, but without me, the therapist, being the provider of that touch. It can be so healing. Remember Josh saying that he didn't remember ever being held by his real mother? Then he asked to be held by his Ideal Mother. She *turns and wraps both arms around him, drawing him to her, with one hand gently holding his head to her chest. He snuggles right into her, holding her tight. During the ten or twelve minutes when he cuddled into her, much of it in silence, the whole group could see that he was drinking in the nourishment on a body level. "God! That felt marvellous," he said, clearly feeling satisfied.*

Trauma is held in the body

When, like Chloe, the client has a trauma reaction, it is such a body-based, physical experience that the most effective 'reset' will also be body-based, to correct the hyper-arousal. In Chloe's structure she went through many different stages, and we saw various kinds of physical contact.

Initially, she needed a Contact Figure, someone in the 'here and now' whose job was to give support whilst she felt the 'big' feelings. Then she had Protection Figures, who would have been in the 'there and then' of her childhood, protecting her. I think they made her feel safer. Only when she began to feel safe was she able to feel a body symptom. She said, *"My shoulders are really aching."* She felt protected enough to begin to feel an impulse (for action), but not yet safe enough to express that impulse, hence the ache.

When I invited her to see what her shoulders wanted to do, *she raised her shoulders and shortened her neck*, as if shrinking out of sight. It seemed that Chloe was just at the verge of further expression, but something inside was stopping her. By providing a Resistance Figure, pushing down on the tops of her shoulders, to support the part of *her* that had been stopping the expression, *she* no longer needed to hold it back from the inside. This gave space to another part of her, the part that was wanting to communicate something. Not only this, but when the Resistance Figure pushed down, she had to put more effort into raising her shoulders. With this added focus and effort, she fully experienced the impulse of those muscles to lift her shoulders. *This connected her to the underlying feelings.*

Once she connected to her previously suppressed feelings, she was able to express them in the form of a scream. That brought her fear into her awareness, so that it could be named, and welcomed, by her Ideal Mother who hugged her saying, *"If I had been your Ideal Mother when you were a child, I would have held you whilst you felt your fear. It would have been safe for you to feel your fear with me,* *and I would have helped you handle all your feelings."* The fear was no longer held inside and hidden. Chloe had accessed the energy and could integrate it. I imagine that the scream had been sitting in her body for a long time, waiting to come out.

Abuse can leave us excessively vulnerable

Excessive vulnerability and openness can be the result of abuse. By abuse I mean any transgression of boundaries. This could be physical: rape, violence, or even surgical intervention as a child. Or it could be psychological abuse: being yelled at or being shamed. The client feels defenceless and exposed. Some people who have been abused develop a survival mechanism of appeasing. As Al Pesso has observed,[7]

> "One of the most unexpected and surprising findings in our work has been that abuse of any kind, physical, psychological or sexual, produces a reflexive, erotic element. The person under attack not only responds with defensive reactions, but may also experience reflexive bodily impulses, not immediately available to consciousness, that imply a readiness to receive penetration... Of course in sexual abuse this element is even further heightened. Not that she wants or consciously feels any sexual excitement, but the sexual organs are involved and some unconscious part of her reacts to this stimulation. This only adds to her distress because she has not asked or wanted to be stimulated. She has been denied her rights to have mastery over her own feelings and body."

It is common for a person who has been sexually abused, whether male or female, to want to close themselves up. Yet often a part of them over which *they do not have conscious control* moves in the opposite way, opening up. In Chloe's structure we saw this when her legs started to tremble, caused by the conflicting desires: to open and close.

Providing safe boundaries

Chloe was also able to work, through touch, with boundaries and limits. In a group clients can physically test boundaries, and experience them being held. As my teacher, Lowijs Perquin said,[8]

> "Together with the technique of explicitly establishing a therapeutic climate… and the principle of creating an alternative symbolic event (Antidote), the technique of physical limiting in a therapeutic context is the most important contribution of PBSP to the field of psychotherapy."

Two Limiting Figures, women, were brought in to hold an absolute boundary. They did this by holding Chloe's knees, keeping her legs completely closed and together. This was with Chloe's conscious agreement. It was vital that Chloe never felt trapped, but instead felt safely contained.

We were not restricting her defences, but were containing and limiting her openness to further abusive contact, and the (often unconscious) desire to appease and submit to the abuser. Chloe experienced safe limits, which allowed her to attend to, experiment with, and integrate the desire to open. This released a huge amount of energy. Later Chloe said she had felt a sense of safety to know that however hard she tried she could not separate her legs, and open herself inadvertently.

Discovering that you cannot break through a boundary that you previously believed was weak and unsafe, is an extraordinary experience. You need real people to hold the boundary, and you must put all your strength into breaking through it, to discover, for yourself, that it really will not give way. Remember Sheila in Chapter 4, who experienced limits that were safely, and completely, held by her Ideal Father. In the safe context of the group, she pushed him as hard as she could. Despite fully expressing her power and rage she couldn't overpower her Ideal Father. Furthermore, he sanctioned her fury and her strength. She could see that *if* he had been her Ideal Father, he really could have handled it all. Putting that experience back in time (to the childhood place where it was needed) allowed her to more fully accept and own her power and aggression. Both Sheila and Chloe had a symbolic experience *at the same time* as a real, truly felt, literal experience of healthy boundaries.

It is worth noting here that interventions requiring physical limits are almost impossible in one-to-one therapy. They simply cannot be done in the imagination because any client who needs to test a boundary has a deep-seated belief that they can, if they really try, overpower the other.

Integrating and unifying polarities

A structure which tests limits enables the client to integrate and unify opposites and polarities. One such polarity is power and vulnerability. Chloe's personal power had been violated by her abuser. This had left her, throughout her life, too open and vulnerable. Because, in the structure, she had two people holding her legs completely closed, thus giving her 'a limit', a dependable boundary she was unable to break through, she was able to put all her energy into trying to open. This allowed her to experiment with, own and integrate her desire to open voluntarily, in a completely safe context, so that the option (of opening) could become a part of her natural behaviour. This also allowed her to assimilate the opposite impulse, which was to close. I noticed in later sessions that her voice had grown stronger, and she expressed herself with a greater natural authority. This was different from the start of the session, when her vulnerability showed in both her voice and eyes. *She was pulling me in to hear her words, rather than speaking them out into the room,* and *one could fall into her eyes.* Through her structure, she had integrated more of her vulnerability, and gained more access to her power, giving her access to more of herself.

Giving the client control
Wherever there are abuse issues it is vital that the client is given control of every step. During every structure it is important to keep the client's pilot, the executive decision-making part of them, present and awake. But it is *particularly* important in any kind of abuse where the person has been violated and lost control over what happened to them. Throughout the session with Chloe I checked every word and every step, to ensure that she was in charge both of what happened, and of the pace at which it happened.

Chapter 6

Peter and Anita

Sex is like oxygen, you don't worry about it
until you aren't getting enough.

Peter and Anita are in their forties, and had met through mutual friends nine years previously. It had been an instant attraction, and they had quickly decided that they wanted to be together. Peter is dark, solid, and fairly certain of himself. Anita is dark, shorter, plump and earnest. Dan, their son, is seven years old.

"We are here about our sex life," Peter says boldly, when I ask what they have come for. "It used to be good, but now it has stopped." That is all he says. This seems to be his main motivation for coming.

I look at Anita, "And you? What do you hope to get from coming here?"

"Well, I think there are many parts of our relationship that aren't working well. But yes, the sex is one of them. I am not as interested as I used to be. But over the last few years, Peter has become quick to anger. I find him so unattractive when he shouts, and I really don't want to be with him in the bedroom when he's like that. We don't really talk anymore. I miss that. I feel like Peter only touches me when he wants sex, and I want more than that. I am not just there for his pleasure."

"Which do you want to look at first?"

Peter jumps in, "Sex."

"Okay," says Anita, more slowly.

I find myself thinking, *Peter is more interested in talking about this than Anita. But she said yes, so I'll go along with it.* I assume that the sexual problem is that Anita has lost interest, but later I will find out there is more to it than that – as is so often the case.

"When was the last time you made love?" I ask. They look at one another. Neither answers for a while, then,

"I'm not sure," Peter says, his resonant voice filling the room.

"Not that long ago," Anita chips in.

"Months? Years?" I ask. I wonder what they are going to say… six months ago? Two years ago? Or as one couple once told me, twenty-five years ago.

"We last tried probably four months ago," Peter says. I note the 'tried' which implies that maybe they didn't succeed. Peter looks questioningly at Anita, "And then four months before that? I guess we have had sexual contact three times this year?"

"More than that," she retorts defensively. "More like six."

"Has it always been like that?" I ask

"It was fine at the beginning, for the first eighteen months. Then it started to tail off. Dan was born when we had been together for two years, but sex stopped pretty much while Anita was pregnant, and I guess we haven't really got back into it since then."

This is a very normal pattern. The amount of sex that a couple have at the start of their partnership often bears no relationship to the frequency once the 'honeymoon phase', which lasts somewhere between six months and two years, is over. It is only then that you discover what the 'normal' sex drive is for each individual.

"I'm going to ask you both a question, and I want you each to come up with a figure. But don't change it when you hear what the other one says. Is that okay?" If they are emotionally-fused, the risk is that whoever goes second will adapt their answer to be similar to the other's.

They nod.

"In your ideal world, if the relationship is going well, how often would you like to make love? Peter?" This question helps me to establish the level of each person's sex drive. Peter says ideally twice a week, though once every five days would be alright. Anita says once every week or so, though once every ten days would be okay for her. I breathe a sigh of relief. The work is much harder when there is a big discrepancy. This time the difference is not great. I remember one couple where the woman wanted intercourse four times a week and the man wanted it once every three to four months. That was difficult. In this case I feel reassured, *So far so good.*

"What stops you from making love more often?"

Anita looks at Peter, and he nods, and she says, "Well, I am not that interested any more. And Peter..." she hesitates.

Peter continues, suddenly looking awkward, "I lose my hard-on."

I hadn't expected that. From what they were saying, I had thought that it was Anita's issue. Now I am curious, and I wonder if Anita will want more sex when Peter's erection problems are sorted out. I decide to talk to Peter about his erection. If he is willing, maybe I can help him resolve the physical part of the problem first. Then, later on, the three of us can look at the psychological aspects, to see what else is getting in the way of good sex for them both.

"Can you get a hard-on when you want to?" I ask, reflecting his words back to him.

If clients don't raise the issue of sex, then I always ask about it, in the first or second session. I think *all* therapists, whether they work with couples or with individual clients, should ask, "How is your sex life?" The client may or may not choose to tell us at that stage, but at least it lets them know that it is okay for them to talk about sex when they are ready. I have heard therapists say, "I wait for the client to raise issues around sex." I think that is remiss. It's very difficult for clients, particularly in general, one-to-one therapy where sex and relationships are not the overt focus of the work, to raise these issues. A study in 2015 found that 45% of people in Britain are unhappy with their sex lives.[1]

Peter tells me that for the last two years his erection has been pretty good first thing in the morning, and he can get a strong erection when they start to make love, but that he quite often loses it just as he is about to penetrate. "The doctor prescribed me pills which worked, but I don't want to take them. I don't like taking pills anyway, and they made my vision go blue round the edges – it was too disconcerting."

"Ah, Viagra or Cialis. One of my clients told me how much he loved the 'blue' vision; as he said, 'Then I know it is definitely working!'"

"Well I don't like taking aspirin even if I have a headache. So I don't know what to do. I don't like it that my penis doesn't work properly, I don't feel like a proper man if I can't get it up."

For some men, sexual problems will go right to the very heart of their masculinity. "At least one in ten men has a regular problem with their hard-on," I tell him. Then I check, "Did the doctor undertake a thorough medical check? Testing you for things like diabetes, cardiovascular problems, and checking your testosterone levels?" Erection problems can be an early warning signal for heart disease, preceding a cardiovascular event, in some men, by two to five years,[2] so I always ensure that the doctor has done a thorough check of the client's heart, as well as taken blood tests to eliminate other physical causes for erection problems.

Peter says that he has a great doctor, who had tested everything and the results had come back as normal.[3]

"If you get an erection but then lose it, have you thought about using a cock ring?"

Peter goes quiet, and then asks, "How does that work?"

"When you have an erection, the penis fills with blood, through the arteries. This is what makes you hard. After you have ejaculated, the blood flows out through veins, and the penis becomes soft. You have what is called 'venous leakage', where the blood leaves the penis too early, via the veins.

"There are two types of rings. One type is called a cock ring. It is like a strong rubber band with handles, and it goes at the base of the penis. You use an applicator to put it onto your already-hard penis, as soon as you get the erection. There are various sizes of ring, so you find one that creates a snug fit, keeping the blood in your penis, which makes your erection last. When you want to remove it, simply pull the two handles; this allows blood to flow out of the penis, so you lose your hard-on."

I pause, to check how they are taking this. Peter is sitting upright, leaning slightly forward. *He's keen,* I think. Anita looks at me, and then at him. *She's hard to read,* I think. *I wonder what she's thinking?*

"The other kind is called a penile scrotal ring, also known as a cock and ball ring, which goes on *before* the erection starts. You put one testicle through first, then the second testicle, and then bend the flaccid penis and put that through. It fits snugly against the body behind the testicles. The arteries are deeper in the body, the veins are closer to the surface. With this ring the blood can flow in through the arteries, but cannot leak out again through the veins, so your penis stays hard. You can buy metal versions of these, but start with a rubber one. They are inflexible, but if you use the wrong size, and it is too tight, with rubber you can cut it off if you need to! You shouldn't leave either ring on for more than thirty minutes. They both work well to keep an erection in place. I would try both types, but maybe start with the cock ring, and see how that goes?"

Peter is engaged now. "I had heard of those, but haven't tried them. I didn't know they would work for me."

I advise him not to buy a cock ring from a typical sex shop, but to get one from a medical device manufacturer.[4] This is because you need to get a good fit (to keep the blood in the penis), and the medical ones come with a selection of sizes and an applicator and, in my experience, sex shops tend to only stock one size. Cock and ball rings, on the other hand, are generally available in all three sizes in most sex shops, because they are simple rubber rings. *They are like the old hoover rings,* I think to myself, *only smaller.* They are not expensive, so I suggest he buys all three to start with, so he can experiment and find the right size. "Do you think you might try it? I know you don't like the idea of pills, so how do you feel about this?"

"I think that might be okay. I'll give it a go and let you know."

"Anita," I check. "How do you feel about Peter using a cock ring?"

"I am not sure," she replies. "We need to sort out other bits too; his angry bouts, Peter not talking to me." It is clear that Anita and Peter also have relationship issues that will need tackling, to help the sexual side of their relationship.

"Okay, let's talk about that now. What happens when you try to talk to Peter?"

Peter interrupts, "I think that if the sexual issue was sorted out I might not be so angry. Can we leave discussing my anger until another time?" I wonder if this is true, but feeling slightly sceptical I nod, agreeing to let them see how it goes. I know that if there is more to this anger, then it will emerge again in another session, so I am willing to follow Peter's lead on that for now.

But Anita brings up the communication issue again. "Apart from the issue around anger and arguing, I'd like us just to talk more," she says.

"What about?" asks Peter defensively.

Anything," says Anita. "I just feel we are drifting apart, that I don't know you as well as I want to any more. I don't feel you know me!"

"Well, there are some things that I don't understand about you," Peter says. Anita looks curious. "Take last week when we went shopping. You tried on that blue and yellow dress, and it looked absolutely lovely on you. I offered to buy it for you, but you said no." He turns to me. "It's often like that. She doesn't seem to want the things I want to give her." I point back to Anita, indicating he should be talking to her, not to me. That way they can 'practise' talking, and it gives me a chance to see the dynamics between them. I want to understand how they get into problems when they talk about difficult things.

Anita says, "Well, actually I did like the dress. I really did. But it cost over a hundred pounds, and that just seemed too much."

"But we've got the money," Peter said, peevishly. "We are both working. We are very lucky. There is only Dan to worry about. I see you buying things for Dan, but you don't spend money on yourself – you *can't* spend money on yourself. You can't let *me* spend money on you either. It seems a shame."

Defensively Anita responds, "This isn't what I want to talk about!"

"Ah, so we have to talk about what *you* want to talk about, do we? Maybe that is why we don't talk. Unless it is what *you* want to discuss then you aren't interested."

A good point, I find myself thinking.

"No, it isn't that," she says. "It's just that I want us to be closer."

Now he is getting frustrated. "But if I can understand what makes you tick, then we will be closer. This is me trying to get closer to you."

I intervene. "There does seem to be some truth to that. Maybe we should talk about this for a bit, and then find something that you want to talk about afterwards, Anita? Or, if we run out of time today, then you can choose the topic next time?"

"Okay. Well, I guess I don't know why I didn't buy the dress… or let you buy the dress for me. I regret it, but I don't know why. That's why I don't want to carry on talking about this, because I don't feel like it will take us anywhere. I don't understand it myself."

"It sounds like it feels too difficult to work out what was going on, so a part of you gives up?"

Anita nods. "It makes me feel too vulnerable, I guess."

I carry on, "A core part of intimacy is being willing to confront ourselves, and then to reveal that 'newly discovered' self to our partner. This requires a kind of vulnerability. Sometimes people associate vulnerability with being exposed, or with weakness." I look at her to see if she responds, and she nods. I continue, "But there is a robust vulnerability that creates a certain kind of strength." I pause to see how this is landing.

"I think that we both need more of that," says Peter. "We have got good at protecting ourselves, pussy-footing around a bit, and I want to try to be more open."

I wonder aloud, "Maybe that is a good way of thinking about it: openness rather than vulnerability?"

"I can see that what you are saying is real and true," says Anita. "That is what I want. I think. For us to be real with one another. But I honestly don't know why I don't let myself have those treats." Anita looks frustrated and I am not sure whether she is crosser with me, with Peter or with herself. "It isn't just as easy as saying I will, because I know that I still won't."

"Maybe it is hard for you to receive?" I ask. Peter looks at Anita, who turns to me and they both give a small nod.

"Well, yes. It is hard for me to spend money on myself, but I have no problem spending it on Dan or Peter."

I am aware that we only have a few minutes left. "We need to look at that more next time, to work out what stops you from spending on yourself. We are coming to the end of our session now. Can you reflect on it between now and next session, and see what insights come? Make a note of them, and let us know at the next session?"

Anita nods, agreeing.

"Although this conversation was difficult, it is probably the kind of exchange that you need to have, to bring you closer. Is that what you are wanting, Anita, when you say you want to be talking more?"

Anita hesitates. "Yes, I guess it is." She sounds unsure and unconvinced. I wonder if she is wanting me to comment on this, but because of the time I let it go, even though a part of me would love to keep going and understand what she is wanting to communicate. There might be something important to talk about, but the session is over, and I have another couple coming.

"These conversations are challenging, because they require both of you to look at yourselves honestly, and admit the things that you have been avoiding. It is okay *not* to know why you feel like you do, but the important thing is to step into that discomfort of not knowing, and sit with it rather than avoiding it. I guess you have to be willing to give it a go. You took a step in that direction today, Anita. Just as Peter did…" I turn now, directing my words to Peter, "When you talked about your erections. It's uncomfortable, but that is where the progress lies, the growth. We're out of time for today. Sometimes I set homework, but I am not going to set specific homework today. But I am aware that you might surprise me! Peter, you look like you might get the cock ring and try it before I see you? Anita, I do want you to reflect on this issue of finding it hard to let Peter buy you things. Maybe you might have a go at talking together too? I look forward to next time, and hearing how it goes. It would be good if there is some news with the cock rings, and with the talking!"

Peter and Anita: Eight Weeks Later

Love is not measured by how many times you touch each other,
but by how many times you reach each other.
Unknown

Peter is pleased. "The cock ring works well. I set it up on the applicator by the side of the bed, and when I get an erection, pop it on and… Bob's your uncle! My penis gets a bit colder, but it is fine. I get a good erection. All is good, and I much prefer it to taking a pill every time I want to make love." He is smiling broadly, and looks proud. *He is sounding proud to be a man again,* I think to myself.

It is two months later, and they have had four therapy sessions. Anita has been honest and told me that although she is masturbating about once a week, she isn't that interested in sex with Peter. I wonder what might be contributing to that. They both say they are talking more than they did, and they seem to be generally friendlier with one another. So it doesn't seem to be a relationship issue any more.

I briefly wonder how Anita would rate the quality of their sex life, because people only *want* sex, when the sex is *worth wanting*! Anita says she has an orgasm from time to time, and that isn't a problem for her. But I wonder.

Then I ask myself, *is the issue a lack of arousal?* At the start of a relationship each person makes a big effort to please the other, and then, as time passes, they cut the foreplay back to the minimum.

She might have worked out that he doesn't like it when she kisses his nipples, so she stops doing that. He discovers that she doesn't like her ears to be nibbled so he stops doing that. Sometimes couples cut back so much on the 'extras' that they drop below a threshold, and there is no longer enough stimulation to get fully aroused. But I don't think that is the issue with Anita and Peter. She says she gets wet, and lubrication is not a problem for her. She has told me she is masturbating once a week, so her sex drive is okay. I begin to think that even if they had fantastic sex, Anita wouldn't be that interested. I feel baffled. I wonder, *What is the underlying issue that could be causing this problem?*

I ask them to talk more about their past, about their sexual history as well as about their childhood. Anita begins to share something that feels very significant to me, and I feel irritated with myself that I didn't spot the signs of this before. There were hints pointing to this in our earlier sessions, but I missed them. Two of the main clues lie in the strength of compassion and devotion she feels for her father, and in her difficulty in receiving from others. These indicate that Anita may be in something we call, in PBSP, a 'Magical Marriage'.

Anita tells me about her very special relationship with her Dad. He used to pick her up from school four days a week. She describes the burst of excitement at looking down the line of parents, and seeing him there. She says, "We had the best of relationships. Dad and I used to sit on the sofa together, whilst Mum would sit separately, in an armchair." As she talks about her father, her voice and her body soften. "I think Mum was jealous of our relationship," she says. "It must have been hard for her, because now I think back, I think it was me and Daddy against Mummy."

Peter chips in. "I hadn't realised that about you before, not in quite that way." His face reddens and his tone changes, and he seems aggrieved. "I think that this is happening a bit with you and Dan, the same thing. He seems to be more important to you than I am."

"It sounds like that really hurts you?" I suggest.

Peter tears up. I have touched a raw spot.

"Ouch," I say softly, acknowledging his pain. I wait a moment, for him to really connect to his feelings, and, when I sense he has moved on a bit, I say, "Yes, we will need to come back to that." This issue with Dan is important, and I make a mental note to raise it again in a later session. However, I am intrigued to check out the relationship between Anita and her father, as I think this may be the underlying problem. Working on this might help the sexual issue, and may also help to free up the issue with Anita and Dan.

It seems that, as a child, Anita thought that her father's relationship with her mother was unsatisfactory. Anita, trying to be helpful, had stepped in to be a 'little wife' for her dad. The problem for the child who has this special bond, this 'Magical Marriage', is that it is almost impossible to get a divorce. When the child becomes an adult, the fact that they are still (at an unconscious level) inappropriately bonded with their parent-as-a-partner will often profoundly affect their intimate relationships.

There are three patterns that I see in those who, as children, had a Magical Marriage with a parent. Some don't form a strong bond with their adult partner – in which case it is the partner's complaints that alert me to this. Some form a stronger relationship with their own child (as Anita was doing with Dan, creating a 'new' Magical Marriage with her son). The third group find that their 'proper' adult relationships are not very sexual, once the honeymoon period is over. Sex may have been fine at the start in the 'new' relationship, but once they settle into familiarity, it is almost as if they don't want to be unfaithful to their 'first marriage' (which was with Mum or Dad). Occasionally, as with Anita, I'll see two or three of these patterns simultaneously.

I know only one way to 'get divorced' from a Magical Marriage, and that is the process I will go through with Anita today. I begin to explain: "A Magical Marriage is often an unconscious thing. In your case, you were aware that there was a special bond between you and your dad. That's a good start, as often people don't even have this level of awareness. But it's important for you to understand that at some level your compassion was awoken for your father when you were just a child, and a part of you 'stepped out' to take care of him in some way. Does that fit?"

She pauses, thinking, then slowly says, "Yes, I would be the one who would listen to him about his work struggles. We were the ones that had physical affection – I don't know whether Mum and Dad were making love, but I doubt it. I never saw him kiss her, or hold hands with her, or even give her a cuddle." She looks surprised. "No, I never ever saw them touch!" It seems that this is the first time she has realised this. "Poor Dad."

"There it is, your compassion for your father. You are feeling it now." I think to myself, *She didn't say 'poor Mum!' It is just her father that awakens this compassion.*

Anita nods, looking bleak.

"There is a step we can do. Are you up for it?"

"Okay," she says, curious and cautious.

"I want you to choose an object," I get up and find my box of buttons, shells, stones and bits and pieces, and some cushions of different sizes and shapes, "to represent your Father-as-a-Young-Man."

She chooses a small, square, ruby-coloured cushion.

"Place him somewhere."

She puts him right next to her foot.

"So this," I point at the cushion "represents your real Father-as-a-Young-Man. How interesting. You have put him right next to you, which is where clients often place people they are looking after or feel responsible for!" I pause, so she can take this in.

Before I can continue, she says, "Yes, I have always felt that he needed looking after."

"So this is an indication that we are right on track. I am going to ask you to move the cushion a bit further away. Is that okay?"

She nods, compliant, and moves the cushion representing him a few feet away. When I feel into her, as Anita, I am humouring Juliet a bit. Back to Juliet, I think, *Oops she's only doing this because I asked her to,* and I hope that will start to change in the next five minutes. *I don't want her to do this for me, but to do it for herself. On the other hand, she doesn't really know what we are doing yet, so I guess it is understandable that she is humouring me!*

"Now we are going to give him," I point to her father, "an Ideal Wife. The kind of wife that he really needed. Could you choose an object to represent his Ideal Wife?"

She goes to the pile and chooses a cushion that is about the same size as the ruby one, but this one is covered with gold and green embroidered velvet, very luxuriant and beautiful. To me, this is a good sign. She has chosen a beautiful cushion of a similar size, indicating that she is ready for someone else more fitting than her to take on her role with her father. She is ready to hand it on.

"Now find a place for his Ideal Wife," I encourage, pointing to the golden cushion.

She puts it down about two feet away from the cushion representing her father.

"Gosh, that is a long way away. Is that how you think it should be for your father, or is that how it was in your real history, when you were a child?"

"That is more how it was," she says.

"Remember, this is the *Ideal* Wife for him."

"Okay, yes. In that case they could be closer to each other."

I move quickly, squatting on the floor behind these cushions-representing-people. I bring the cushion representing the Ideal Wife close to her Real Father, so that they are touching. "Is that okay?" I check.

She nods. "What did your father need from an Ideal Wife?" I ask.

She answers straight away, without hesitation. "Someone who would be there for him. She would be loving, and interested in him."

In front of her, Anita has a clear view of an imaginary movie screen, and I am behind it to 'choreograph the show' with these two figures. I pick up the cushion representing the Ideal Wife for Anita's real father, and, moving it up and down a few inches, I make it look like she is talking to Anita's father.

I say (and I am looking at the object-representing-Anita's-real-father as I say this), "'If I had been your Ideal Wife,' she says to him, 'I would have been there for you. I would have been loving and I would have been interested in you.'" Then I look up at Anita to see her reaction.

"Yes, that's good. She would have paid him attention when he came home from work," Anita says.

I pick up the Ideal Wife again, so that she says to (the object representing) Anita's father: "'If I had been your Ideal Wife, then I would always have given you attention when you came home from work.'"

"She'd have asked how his day went," Anita says.

"'I would have said to you,' she says to him, 'How did your day go? What happened today?'"

Anita breathes out. "Oh god, that would have been soooo good."

"What else did he need? What did *you* do for him?" I ask.

"Affection," says Anita.

I pick up the Ideal Wife again, "'If I had been your Ideal Wife, I would have been affectionate with you. We would have held hands, and cuddled.'"

"Y-e-s! God… She could have been there for him and I wouldn't have needed to be."

"Exactly," I respond. "Then the Ideal Wife for your father comes out of the movie, and she looks directly at you, and she says to *you*…" and I turn the Ideal-Wife-for–her-real-father round to face her, and make it seem as if the Ideal Wife is speaking to *Anita*: "'*I* would have been there for him. *I* would have paid attention to him, listened to him, been affectionate and loving with him as a wife, and held hands and cuddled with him as a wife. That would have been *my* job. *Not... your... job.* **My** job. And *I* would have loved him, as a wife does.'" Then I turn the Ideal Wife back to face Anita's father.

Anita lets out a huge sigh of relief, and as I feel into her, things are a bit different. I am looser than earlier, there is much less tension in my body. Energy is flooding through me. Then coming back to my own body, as Juliet, I want to help Anita to notice this change. I ask her, "What is happening in your body?"

"Well, it feels fantastic. I can breathe in a way that I haven't for years. I tend to have a bit of asthma, and often I can't take a full breath. But I feel like I can now." She takes a full breath, as if experimenting with how deeply she can inhale.

"That's interesting, because Al Pesso[5] has noticed over the years of doing this work that breathing issues are often related to father issues. This is all about releasing you from the burden of responsibility around your father."

"I feel like a weight has been lifted. I feel lighter."

"So the Ideal Wife would turn to you again, and say, 'It's *my* job to love him like a wife, and you could just have been a little girl. *I* would have been there for him as a wife. It's *my* job, not *your* job.'"

Anita gives a huge sigh again, and leans back in her chair. This sitting back is a sign I often see at this stage. It indicates a shift in energy. She has been released from an intangible but inappropriate bond.

"And I can imagine the two of them being affectionate together," she says.

"Let's do that piece. But let's change the focus now, and bring some more figures into the room here, so you can place these new memories even more firmly into your sense of your own history. How about having an Ideal Mother who would have been there for you, who would also have been there as an Ideal Wife for your Father? Can you imagine that?" She nods.

"And let's bring in an Ideal Father for *you*, who would have been happy with his wife, and not needed to turn to *you* in that way."

"Nothing sexual ever happened with me and my father," Anita insists.

"No, I understand that. There was no sexual connection, but it was an inappropriate emotional bond." Anita nods, understanding what I am saying.

"Where would you place an Ideal Mother and an Ideal Father, for you, if they were here?"

"I would put them standing behind me, him on the right and her on the left."

"Yes. And how would they be with one another?"

"They would have arms around each other's waists, and they would each have one hand on my shoulder."

"Perfect, just imagine that now. Maybe they say to you, 'If we were your Ideal Parents you would have *seen* us being affectionate with one another, loving one another.'"

Anita leans back, eyes closed, and her face softens and relaxes.

"Maybe you could imagine that the back of the chair represents their legs, and you can lean back against them and feel their support?" I ask. Since we don't have a group to role play the Ideal Parents, I enrol the chair as Ideal Parents.

Anita sighs. "This is big," she says. "I haven't felt this relaxed for ages. I feel lighter, freer, and able to breathe so deeply."

I gesture, indicating that the Ideal Parents are speaking. "'If we had been your Ideal Parents when you were a young child,' they say, 'you could have breathed this deeply with us.'"

A few minutes pass. Peter and I are in a reverent silence. There is a particular quality in the room, it is soft and tranquil. At moments like this I feel the profound peace of the happy child. I notice that Peter's body has relaxed too. He has been completely quiet and still whilst all this has been happening, but as I sense into him, I feel – as Peter – engaged, easy and intrigued about what has gone on and where it has led.

Anita says, in a voice drunk with a quiet pleasure, "I am imagining them, my Ideal Parents, hugging, and I am on the sofa looking at them. It feels *so* good to see that. To imagine them *really* together. I know I could go and join them if I wanted to, and that I would be welcomed."

A few minutes later, Anita shows signs that she is feeling complete. She starts to open her eyes, and blinks a few times. She looks at me, then at Peter, and bursts out laughing. He laughs and tears start to roll down his cheeks, and suddenly I find that I too am full, overflowing with love, and I can't contain it as I watch the way the two of them are looking at one another. A few tears roll down my cheeks, too.

Anita and Peter came regularly for a total of about four months, then returned for a one-off session six months later. Their relationship was solid, friendly, warm and loving. They were having sex every two or three weeks. Peter would have preferred more, but accepted this. The cock ring continued to work well for him, and sometimes they made love without it. Anita told me laughingly, "I am now able to receive his love, and his gifts!" She had learned to prioritise her relationship with Peter, so that he knew he was her number one. Dan was growing up and seemed to be doing well, and they felt content with their family.

Thoughts and Theory: The Magical Marriage

People confuse feeling responsible for someone with being in love with them. It's different.
Rescuing, care-taking or feeling responsible for another person's happiness is not the same as love.

A nita had had a Magical Marriage with her father, a special closeness, a bond that everyone could see. A Magical Marriage can develop whenever there is a gap where the 'spouse' should be, so the child steps in to take care of the other parent in some way. Anita and her father's was overt and clear, but a Magical Marriage can happen in a subtler way, and is often completely hidden.

The covert Magical Marriage

In a covert Magical Marriage, the child may not actually be *doing* anything for their parent in real life. It all happens unconsciously, in the child's imagination. They often grow into adults who do not recognise that they have been in a Magical Marriage. One of my clients, Adam, emphatically told me, "I couldn't have done that with my mother, I didn't particularly like her! Plus, she was living across the other side of the world from when I was five years old." Yet it transpired that he had indeed formed a Magical Marriage with his mother.

Unconsciously, as a young child, Adam had imagined his mother getting treated in the way that she deserved, being loved, cherished and cared for, providing what he thought that his mother was lacking. In Adam's sessions, I noted various indications that there might have been a Magical Marriage. The main clue was the overwhelming compassion that Adam felt when talking about his mother, even though he said he didn't like her. Other clues were: his difficulty receiving, a tendency to depression, and the number of projects that he had started, but never finished. The ultimate test was to create a scene where an object representing his Real-Mother-as-a-Young-Woman (Adam chose an almond in its shell) was given an Ideal Husband (for this he chose a walnut in its shell). I remember Adam sitting staring at the scene, entranced and captivated by his real mother being 'loved and held' by her Ideal Husband. After a while, I said to him, "If you hadn't had a Magical Marriage, then this scene would just be an almond and a walnut. But that is not what you are seeing down there. You are completely engrossed, seeing your mother getting what she needed with her Ideal Husband, who would have loved her in just the way that she wanted, and who would have stayed with her." Adam laughed, as he finally saw the role he had been playing. Only through recognising it, and then having the role filled by someone else (represented by the walnut), was he able to 'get a divorce' from his real mother, and be fully available for his current, adult, intimate relationship.

Anita, too, had constructed an out-of-awareness, virtual wife for her father in her mind's eye. This wife did all the things that she perceived her father needed, things that her mother was not doing. She had done this because she didn't think her mother was caring well enough for certain aspects of her father's needs; this left a gap, so Anita stepped in and did it instead. Sometimes this took place in reality (cuddling up with him, listening to him, being there for him) and at other times covertly, in her imagination. This was different to Adam, who had done it *all* covertly, completely unconsciously.

I know this one well, because I had an overt Magical Marriage with my mother, and a covert Magical Marriage with my father. My father was an intensely private man, and my mother was tactless and tended to blurt out the family secrets. I remember, aged about seven, cringing as she told people when we were going on holiday, something my father hated others to know. I now realise, though I was completely unaware of it at the time, that I must have made a film in my mind's eye, giving my father the wife he needed who would have honoured his privacy and never revealed confidential information. On the other hand, my father was sometimes cruel and often critical of my mother, and I also made films where I provided my mother with a respect and kindness that I thought a husband should offer.

We don't notice that our minds are constantly processing

It fascinates me that so much is going on in our minds that we do not notice – unless we have trained ourselves to do so. You may remember times when you have been talking about something and then, suddenly, have a seemingly unconnected thought. If you mentally retrace your steps then you will find the trail that led from one thought to the other. For example, I am talking about my brother, and I spontaneously remember that I must collect the dry cleaning that I should have picked up yesterday. When I go back over my thinking process, I recall that last time I saw my brother he spilt red wine on his suit and said, "Damn. Now I will have to take this suit to the dry cleaners and I was going to wear it to the interview on Monday." Today, when talking about my brother again, I have unconsciously brought up many images of him in different situations. One of these was the last time I saw him. I re-see, in my mind's eye (but I don't notice that I am seeing this), the moment when he spilt the wine. Then I (unconsciously still) remember him mentioning the dry cleaners. I may even see my local dry cleaners. This prompts me, and I, consciously now, remember that I still need to pick up my dry cleaning.

Research suggests that altruism is innate

Many people think that even small children are altruistic.[6] It seems that we are born knowing what is right and just. Children recognise that adults deserve a good partner, with whom they have a strong bond. We want that for our parents. So if there is any gap in the parental relationship, there is a risk that the child will step in.

This could be a literal gap, when one parent dies, and the child forms a Magical Marriage with the parent that survives. Society colludes with this, for example saying to a six-year-old boy whose mother has died, "You are the man of the house now." More commonly, it may be a symbolic gap, that is created if the parents separate or divorce – the child may 'look after' one or both parents through a Magical Marriage. It can also occur when a parent is seriously ill, and the worried child wants to take care of them. Or, if a parent is violent or cruel to their spouse, the child may step in to protect and support the other parent. On the other hand, as in Anita's case, when the parents' marriage is not good enough (at least in the child's estimation), this can awaken the child's sympathy, concern, and yearning for her father (or mother) to have a better spouse. In other words, *any* situation where there is a 'vacuum' – an absence of the adult fulfilling the role of husband or wife appropriately – can suck the child in, to create a Magical Marriage.

Some parents prioritise their children over their partner

For some adults, parenting consumes all of their energy, and they have little left over for their spouse. Their child becomes the priority, which may unhelpfully 'pull' the child into the role

194

of a partner. It would have been revealing to ask Anita's father, "Which has priority, being a parent or being a partner?" The answer, without a shred of hesitation, should be 'my partner'. In a healthy situation, the love that parents have for their child is the result of their love for one another. When this has gone wrong, it is important to restore the couple relationship to the top priority, and the parent-child relationship to second place. Children feel happiest when they know their parents love one another, and it often improves the parenting too.

Anita intuitively knew that her relationship with her father was stronger than the bond he had with his wife. Her mother recognised that Anita's tie to her husband was more important than her own connection to him, and was jealous. Through this, Anita acquired a sense of primacy, and a greater level of influence and power than she should have had as a child. This inflated her self-esteem and she developed a kind of omnipotence. This manifests as 'I am the one and only who can do this'. This omnipotence is one of the main consequences of both overt and covert Magical Marriages. It will have a profound impact on the child, sometimes negatively affecting them for the whole of their life.

Omnipotence

This omnipotence manifests in people differently. One person might say, 'I am the only one who really knows how to…'. I remember one client who enrolled someone to represent 'The Figure of All Knowledge and All Wisdom' to look after his real mother. But his omnipotence was so great that he felt that even 'All Knowledge and All Wisdom' didn't really know how to look after his mother as well as *he* could! In the end he decided that no one on earth could look after his mother properly, and God was the only one he could trust to do it well. So we brought in someone to represent 'God', and this finally allowed him to step out of the 'God' place himself, letting go of his omnipotence to become merely human. Having made this step, he said he felt a huge relief. He hadn't realised what a burden he had been carrying for all those years.

Another person might play out the specialness through the martyr role: 'I am so giving that *I* am the one that must give to *everyone*.' Or you may see omnipotence displayed in the form of inverse grandiosity: 'I see this working for everyone else, but therapy won't help *me*.' The implication is that 'I am too damaged for anything to work, I am the *only* one who is as damaged as this.' Another client might say, 'I am the *only* one as miserable as this.' One could substitute 'stressed', 'anxious' or 'afraid' for 'miserable'. These clients have an investment in suffering alone, because that is where they have found their uniqueness and specialness. They get stature from their suffering.

Overloaded with feelings
Al Pesso, noting this pattern and the consequences of that omnipotence, describes,[7]

> "When we fill those holes [creating a Magical Marriage] and become *the only*, all hell breaks loose, for our killing forces and our sexual forces are no longer limited, modulated or bound."

He is describing an overload of the feelings of aggression and sexuality, which get released when we are in a Magical Marriage, and again this happens outside the child's awareness. Maybe we know that we have a lot of feelings. However, by and large when we are children, we think that what happens to us is normal, and assume that other children are having similar experiences. We are highly unlikely, when we are young, to be able to attribute the correct emotional labels to these feelings.

Martin Teicher[8] has researched neurobiology and the brain. When he studied the lifelong impact of early maltreatment and neglect, he discovered a link to changes in brain chemistry. Maltreatment and neglect affect the hormones vasopressin and oxytocin, which cause an increased tendency for sexual acting out, aggression and violence. This seems to support what Al Pesso has been talking about for forty years, in relation to Magical Marriages and omnipotence. There is an interesting piece of research to be done on Magical Marriages and the effect on hormones (and what happens during the subsequent filling of that 'gap') – but that goes beyond the scope of this book.

Holes in roles

At this point I want to mention that a Magical Marriage is just one example of the category of 'holes in roles'. 'Holes in roles' refers to any gap or hole in the family system. For example, a 'hole' is created if a parent dies whilst the children are young. If the child feels a lot of concern, then they will be driven by their desire for completion to fill the 'hole'. This is due to our innate preference for wholeness.

Let's imagine a family with two children, where the mother has died. This leaves two obvious 'holes' that a child might fill. One is to take on the 'role' of a mother for their sibling (to replace the dead mother). The second is to take on the 'role' of a wife for their father (to replace the dead spouse). Children fill 'holes in roles' when their compassion is awoken before their basic needs have been met. In my own history, my grandfather (my father's father) was blown up in a gas explosion when my father was just a few weeks old. So, as well as being in a Magical Marriage as my father's 'wife', I also took on the role of 'father for my father'. I was, unconsciously, filling two different 'holes in roles'.

Another point to note here is that 'holes in roles' can go beyond the family. I have known clients to fill a role by 'taking care' of all

197

the starving children in Ireland in the Potato Famine. This task is obviously impossible, but was brought about by hearing stories as a young child of the suffering of the famished children, and wanting to 'make it better'. Another client was unconsciously healing the African Rainforests – or at least trying to. No wonder she was exhausted!

A minority of clients will recognise that they were in a Magical Marriage, though many will find it easier to identify with the ways in which they have (unconsciously) tried to cope with the resulting overload of feelings. There are seven psychological defences[9] which are activated in people who have had a Magical Marriage (or filled any other 'holes in roles').

The psychological defences

Depression

The first is depression. Of course, a Magical Marriage is not the only cause of depression, but it is *one* of the causes. By depressing the vital energies and turning down the thermostat on all feelings, the person is able to shut down the overwhelming flood of feelings in their body.

Disassociation

The second manifestation is through disassociation. This was the pattern we saw with Chloe in Chapter 5, though in her case the cause was trauma, and not 'holes in roles'. The person becomes detached from their experience, and feels as if they are 'outside' of their body; they become numbed or disconnected from their feelings.

Retroflection

The third defence is retroflection. This is when the energy that you want to send outwards is turned back on yourself. One man I worked with said, "As I walk down the high street, I imagine everyone walking towards me is going to punch me in the face." He has taken his anger, projected it out onto others, and thinks they will do to him what he wants to do to them, but is afraid to.

Inability to complete things

The fourth is the inability to complete things. This can be as simple as starting projects but not finishing them, having unconsciously turned off the capacity to complete even simple ordinary closures. Because of our innate drive for wholeness, which brings pleasure and happiness, Pesso[10] links this inability to complete things with an inability to feel fully satisfied and happy with life. He also links it to passive aggressive behaviours, where one is frustrating one's own closures, as well as those suggested by others.

Inability to receive

The fifth is an inability to receive. This applies to everything from accepting compliments, to taking in love. We saw Anita inadvertently undermining her relationship with Peter, not by withholding affection, but by neglecting to accept his tokens of love. This denies Peter the natural pleasure of giving. In the long run, her behaviour stifles any kind of meaningful exchange.

Shame and Guilt

The sixth and seventh are excessive guilt or shame, which may be used in an attempt to hold down and bind the overload of feelings.

These defences can fail

Of course, sometimes those internal defences fail and the individual may then resort to sexual acting out and acts of violence, or at the furthest extreme, even rape and murder. This can also happen on a grander scale: witness innumerable terrorist attacks and unjust wars carried out by those who are still living with a sense of omnipotence of which they are not aware.

Therapists also fill 'holes in roles' in their own lives
It is worth noting that many therapists and people in the helping professions may also have had a Magical Marriage or filled other holes in the roles in the family system. They may tend to take care of others and find it harder to take things in for themselves! At least, that is, until they have had some personal healing around this.

Magical Marriages are Tiring
Magical Marriages are extremely tiring for the child-who-grows-up-to-be-an-adult, filling a hole in a role. Sustaining this role of virtual-wife-for-her-father continually (and unconsciously), draws energy from Anita, both as a child, and as she grows into an adult. It is like a parasite which lives on its host, draining Anita's resources, regardless of whether the parent is alive or dead.

Solving the problem of a Magical Marriage
Getting a divorce from this relationship with one's parent, be it conscious or unconscious, is very difficult to do. PBSP is the only way I know of doing this. We fill the 'hole' by creating a symbolic 'film' to counter the original film that was unconsciously made by the child. Remember, it has to be completely believable to the client. They need to be convinced that the Ideal Wife or Ideal Husband filling the role would have done a better job than they could have done. It is only when the newly-created scene completely fills the 'gap', that they can step back, breathing a sigh of relief as they allow someone else to 'do the job' instead of them.

Filling the 'hole' allows the energies to come back into the client's body

We saw how engaged Anita was, as soon as I brought in the Ideal Wife for her real father. Once she had heard the healing statements, spoken by the Ideal Wife, Anita relaxed. 'Oh, that would have been sooo good', she said. When she truly felt satisfied that her Father was being *properly* taken care of by someone else, she said, 'I can breathe in a way that I haven't for years.' Energy flooded back into her body, and later, as she realised that the burden had gone, she said, 'I feel like a weight has been lifted. I feel lighter.' Al Pesso talks about this:[11]

> "When the clients 'see' those 'movies' in the therapy session, their own energies shift dramatically. They are no longer *the only*, no longer God-like, the unbound forces of aggression and sexuality are now limited, bound and modulated."

We see this as the client sighs and sits back, a sign that energies are being redistributed around their own body, and they will generally find that they have more vitality available on a daily basis. Being human, and accepting ourselves as human, with all our inherent limitations and imperfections, is what this journey of life is all about. Relationships challenge us, and through these challenges, they offer us the opportunity to develop and grow.

Chapter 7

Horses, Therapy and Relationships: Juliet's Story

Be yourself; everyone else is already taken.
Oscar Wilde

I first learnt what I know about people through my contact with horses. As a child I loved all animals, especially horses. Every week or two, my parents would patiently drive me across London to Hampstead Heath so that I could learn to ride. In my teens we found a riding school nearer home, in Osterley, West London. Soon, Mr Ellingham, the riding-school owner, allowed me to become a 'helper', working in exchange for free rides. I would go every day during the holidays, and at weekends, devoting all my spare time and energy to the horses.

The horses

Neon was my favourite, an ugly Appaloosa with a wall eye and a roman nose. Maybe the fact that I have a 'lazy eye' that sometimes wanders made me sympathetic to him. I spent hours washing and grooming him. I would lovingly clean his saddle and bridle – I always put extra effort in if it was Neon's tack, even using a matchstick to clean out each hole in the stirrup leathers!

Yogi Bear was a cobby dark chestnut who set me my biggest tests in horse management. He used to lie down and roll right over in any big patch of mud, ignoring the thwack of my whip and my desperate shouts. I was pink-faced and embarrassed every time I had to ride this muddy pony back to the stable yard.

What did the horses teach me? Above all, the extraordinary power of communication and harmony. Here, QC was my greatest teacher. He was 16.3 hands high (so he was big!), I was in my thirties and together we attended loads of dressage competitions, did some eventing, and even won prizes in a few three-day events.

One of my eventing teachers, Danny Anholt, taught dressage and show-jumping. For the dressage he was brilliant and taught me so much, but it didn't work so well for the show-jumping. He was such a talented jumper that he didn't need to think about what he was doing because it came so naturally to him, which made it harder for him to explain it to me. I struggled. Lacking the natural instinct for jumping, I would often set the horse up wrong for a fence. A good rider will 'see their stride' some five strides away, and be able to encourage the horse to either take slightly longer steps, or shorter bouncy strides, so that he arrives at the optimal take-off point before the jump. Riders who set their horses up well can, in the final moments before take-off, sit very quietly, supporting their horse as he finds the easiest way to get over the fence successfully. I, on the other hand, found it hard to see a stride, which meant that I often interfered with the horse too much just before the jump, trying to correct the error that a good rider would simply have avoided.

I felt ashamed that I wasn't better at jumping. But I persevered. Somewhere in my childhood I had learnt a kind of stubbornness which has served me. I tried a different teacher, Terry Allen, for the jumping, which helped; I kept Danny for the dressage. Terry was good at breaking the process down, so that I could learn the necessary skills in a step-by-step way, thus developing my instincts. Gradually I improved, though neither show-jumping nor cross-country were ever easy. What kept me motivated was the huge thrill of those moments when both horse and rider were in harmony, and all was going well. Maybe it was even better because it had been hard-won. There was one thing in my favour: I'd inherited my father's sense of rhythm (he was a professional double bass player). This helped over the fences, though it was still hard to see a stride. My jumping had improved, to just about good enough!

Maybe this is partly why my favourite discipline was always dressage, in which horse and rider work together to develop balance, athleticism, cadence, precision and beauty.

I am riding QC, and it is going well. The merest hint of a whisper communicates that I want him to glide over to the right at 45 degrees in a half-pass. I change that whisper a fraction, putting a little more weight onto my right seat-bone and close my fingers around the left rein to create a marginally stronger contact with his mouth. This indicates two things: that he should stop going sideways and now go straight forward, *and* that I want to change pace. I keep a light pressure on the right rein, to let him know that I want him to canter. I squeeze the left rein again, simultaneously squeezing with my right leg, near the girth, and lightly brush with my left leg, moving it three inches forward from where it has been, and QC fluently moves from a trot to a canter with his right leg leading.

The signals for half-pass and canter are so similar that much of the communication is also through intention and a kind of telepathy. When the horse is working at its best, and I am too, the feeling of deep connection and attunement is sensational: an ecstasy, bliss. This only happens when I am fully in my own body (inviting the horse to be fully aware of his too), and present to *this* moment, absorbed in the dance of following and leading, listening and inviting, receiving and giving. It was on the back of a horse that I first learned about the meditative state, a quietness and flow where the inner critic has no place. An empty mind, without chatter, full of openness. Horses were a gateway for me, my first opening to a more 'spiritual' state of being.

Another thing I learned from horses is clarity of intention. If one doesn't know where one is intending to go, and at what speed, then one is very unlikely to get there. This was most obvious when I was show-jumping. If I was not fully committed, then the horse wasn't – QC might run out of the side of the fence or stop dead. Horses provided a true mirror of my own inner state.

All the horses I rode taught me when to lead and when to follow, and about assertiveness. Horses check out their rider to see who is in charge. As herd creatures they like to be guided, to be led by a stallion who tells them what to do and where to go. It makes them feel secure, in the same way that children like to know that a parent has ultimate control. But, just like children, they also push the boundaries. More often than not they are testing, but actually wanting the boundary to be held. *How safe am I here? How strong is this person? Can they really protect me, take care of me, look after me in the way that I need it?* So they will assess their rider, and if a horse picks up doubt, fear, or uncertainty, they may feel threatened. Horses taught me to step into my authority, my assertive self.

Cross-country, the third discipline in eventing, taught me about courage. The poles were fixed, the fences were designed not to fall down if knocked, and the pace was fast. If QC 'left a leg behind' over a fence, not making a clean jump, and as a consequence he stumbled, then I might get catapulted out of the saddle, or QC might fall, in which case I would get caught underneath three-quarters of a ton of horse.

QC was waiting; we were warmed up and ready in the 'starting box' of the cross-country phase. The sun was shining but it wasn't too hot. The ground was good, with just the right amount of 'give' in it. The official started to count me down, blowing his whistle to indicate we could start. I barely needed to squeeze him, just softened the pressure on the reins and we were off, galloping down to the first fence, full of terror and excitement.

But who was in charge, horse or rider? My job was to navigate round the course, which I had walked on foot earlier in the day. QC had never seen the course, so I had to set him up correctly for each fence, to give him the best chance to get over. I was trying to slow him down because, although he didn't know it, the next fence was an aptly-named 'coffin fence'. The first part was a harmless-looking hedge, then hidden behind that, only two strides away downhill, was a ditch with water in. Then it was two strides uphill to the third part of the coffin, another hedge. If I didn't slow him up, then he would be going too fast to jump the ditch safely, and would be unlikely to make it over the second hedge.

The more I tried to slow him, the more he tried to ignore me! Since he was a dozen or more times heavier than me, it was an unequal match, and I was getting desperate, in the middle of a major struggle, in the middle of a cross-country course! Would he trust me, and listen to my insistence that there was something coming up that he should be careful about? He wanted to gallop around the whole course as fast as he could! Standing in my stirrups, I pulled on the reins. He stuck his nose out and set his neck against me, flattening and speeding up slightly. I changed tactics. I sat down, as deeply as I could into the saddle, leant back a bit, and gave two strong, steady pulls. I knew that he would feel this, but he could still choose to ignore it.

He suddenly listened. It had worked. It was as if he had changed channel and we had once again locked on to each other. We were tuned in together anew, and this was confirmed when I noticed him turning one ear turn back towards me. Now he was really listening. We were in sync, with just one stride to go to the first part of the coffin – the hedge. However, despite being spot on for the right take-off point, in his enthusiasm he took a huge jump, taking us too close to the ditch. He momentarily hesitated then bravely leapt, more vertically than forward. *Good old QC and his pogo sticks!* I thought. "Good boy," I said out loud to reassure both of us, trying not to get in the way. I knew he was working it out now, and the best thing for me to do was quietly follow as he found his own way. Because he had jumped more up than forward, I felt his back left foot slip at the edge of the ditch, but he managed to use his other three legs to propel us forward. Then we had one good stride to sort ourselves out before the second hedge, which he judged perfectly. We landed, and we were out of the coffin, galloping on our way. I patted him on the neck, relieved, appreciative and grateful. It was team work at its best, and it felt great.

Horses led me to therapy
Horses literally led me to becoming a therapist. Not having come from a horsey family, I bought my first horses when I was twenty-seven years old: Rosie, a 14.3 hands high, beautiful bay mare, and Rufus, a 12.2 pony. I bought them so that I could teach people how to ride, and they lived in a garden outside the Kingston Gate of Richmond Park. I would ride into the park leading one and riding the other. I met the same regulars each week, and spent an

hour with them, teaching them the right position to sit in, how to do the rising trot, the canter, how to start, steer and stop. During their riding lessons, my clients would talk about their lives, and I heard the most amazing things. If things got difficult or too painful, it was really helpful to say, "Shall we have a trot now?" thus diffusing the situation.

In so many ways, Richmond Park was my first therapy room. I heard extraordinary stories of pain, suffering, affairs, bigamy and transvestitism in the families of the most 'normal' of my clients. I was intrigued by people, and my clients used to say to me, "Juliet, you are such a great listener. You ought to become a counsellor." A few years later, at the age of thirty-three, I signed up at Kingston College of Further Education on a 'Professional Counselling' Diploma course.

I didn't stop working with horses, however, and by this time my first husband R had built me (literally brick by brick) a riding school, which we called Barnfield, on the edge of Richmond Park. It had become a thriving business; I loved teaching horse-riding, and thoroughly enjoyed incorporating what I was learning at college about therapy, into my lessons. When someone was being too kind to a horse, and not holding the boundaries and expectations that they should, I would ask if they did the same in their intimate relationships, and the answer was almost always, "Yes". On the occasions when someone was too sharp with the horse, hitting them unfairly or expecting them to do something that was too difficult, I'd ask, "Does your partner disappoint you too?" We used their relationship with the horse as a mirror for their relationship with their spouse or lover – horses were a perfect metaphor. I was talking to people about their relationships, long before I trained to be a couple counsellor!

As I moved from one-to-one therapy into my work with relationships, my equestrian experience continued to be invaluable. Often a couple needs to be 'held'. There is a lot going on when two people are struggling, and the therapist needs to be willing to be quite strong, while at the same time highly attuned. In my early twenties I used to ride a flighty, three-quarter thoroughbred, grey mare called Mystic. She belonged to M, my boyfriend, and I used to take her down to the Upper Richmond Road, a busy London high street. There were lots of people, lorries, dogs and shops – sights and sounds that were unfamiliar to Mystic. I needed to really 'hold' her in those moments. I kept a firm yet following connection through the reins, my legs embracing her sides, and my seat relaxed yet definite and down into the saddle, so that she could feel me there as a reassuring presence in this new, unexpected and slightly frightening environment. When I was tense, my energy would go upwards, and she would get tense too. The best way to show her I was really *with* her was by dropping my weight down into the saddle and grounding my energy, and then she would be more settled. It is the same when working with a couple. It is important that they know that I have a grounded presence and a firm contact. With a horse, you aim for a steady following contact through the reins to the mouth. With a couple, you need a steady following presence that can 'hold' the unexpected, whilst allowing the freedom to go wherever is needed.

The men in my life
The police are coming. By this time, M and I have been together for five years, and have lived together full time for about three. We have both drunk too much, and have had a row. He lashed out at me, and I dialled 999. He's gone upstairs. A male and a female officer have come, and talked first to me. Then they spoke to him. I don't remember what they said. I wanted them to make him leave – but they'd persuaded him to sleep in the spare room for the night.

I am twenty-two-years old, sitting on the sofa, and my life is out of control. I'm scared, lonely, and I don't know what to do. I can't go back to my parents. My Dad disapproves of M, and my going home will prove him right, so I daren't turn to them for help. There is nowhere to go.

It will be another three years before M and I separate, three years where we rub along amicably enough, more like brother and sister than lovers. By this stage, we have stopped having sex. As he allows me to control him more and more, I increasingly lose my respect for him, and my desire. It is a situation where he can only lose. If he doesn't let me control him he gets grief, and if he does, then I lose respect. This loss of respect is ultimately what split us up.

I meet R just as he is about to go off travelling, and we agree to go to Italy together for one year. We end up on the edge of Lake Garda, where my parents and I had often holidayed while I was growing up. Neither of us speak Italian, and we don't have much money. We plan to start off living on a campsite in a tent, and to find work. But we arrive before Easter and the campsites are not yet open. It is a new world, frightening, and I am feeling lost. I think we both are. That pushes us together, and I lean on him, relying on him to take care of me.

He is gorgeous, and I am amazed that he wants to be with me. He looks good on his pedestal. Quickly he gets work in a nearby restaurant, and I work in a pizzeria with Teresa and Guido, who kindly offer us a home in a not-quite-finished flat. We get used to having no doors and not much furniture. We love it. And three days a week I work in the Pizzeria Da Guido, where I gradually learn Italian. In a myriad of ways, I put R first. I assume that my job is to please him, to look after him, and to make his life easier. That is what I had seen my mother do. I had begun to learn with

M that being controlling doesn't work (though this is still a core strategy in my relationships!). With R the dynamic is different. I feel indebted to him for choosing me – because I feel ugly compared to him. As I see it, if I love him enough I will keep him. There are parts of him that I don't like, but if I ignore those bits, I hope that they will go away or change.

One challenging area is anger. I had learned in my family of origin not to do overt anger, whereas R has no trouble showing anger or rage. If someone takes his parking space he will get out and shake his fist at them, shouting at the top of his voice. I, meanwhile, am hiding in the car, cringing in my seat, or tugging at his sleeve begging him to stop.

I am convinced that the best way is to avoid anger, and be 'nice' (not recognising that I am doing this in a passive aggressive way). R takes the opposite polarity, and overtly expresses his anger and rage, anywhere and everywhere. I know now that had *I* stepped up, and *owned* my own anger, then R would not have had to carry my anger for me. He would have been more likely to find his calmer side.

The years pass, and when after twelve years together, R wants a divorce, I am blown apart and devastated. But being a survivor, I pick myself up, and start to move on with my life. Soon, Frank Kevlin, our couples therapist, helps me to see that I'd put my *commitment* to our relationship *above* all my other feelings.

Looking more honestly at what was really going on, for the first time I see the unhappiness that I had been living with. Now in my mid-thirties, I start to attend workshops and seminars, and really begin my self-development journey. Over the next few years I realise how small I had been, that I'd only been allowing certain parts of myself out into the light of day. I realise I am not as shy as I had thought and, gradually gaining confidence, with a lot of love and support from a huge range of people, I stop restricting myself, and start to blossom.

And now I am with William, who has taught me so much and journeyed far with me. He is a writer, leadership coach and shaman-healer-therapist-poet, though he wouldn't call himself that. We work separately and together in a variety of different settings, running workshops for people who want to enhance their relationships. He brings a different, grounded sensitivity to our life. We make a good team, working on our issues as they arise.

Therapy and therapy trainings

It was whilst I was with R that I started therapy for the first time. I was incredibly lucky to have Frank Kevlin as my first therapist. He was born as Fazal Inayat Khan and was the leader of the International Sufi Movement and teacher of the Sufi way of transcendence (although I did not know this at the time). We worked on my relationship issues with R, as well as my experiences as a child. He introduced me to Neuro-Linguistic Programming (NLP), which put me on the path to becoming a counsellor. My time with him has deeply influenced my work as a couples therapist.

From NLP I learnt many things, the most significant of which was the fact that my perception of the world is not accurate, it is just my perception, and may not be shared by others; I had assumed there was a right and a wrong, and that I was right! But I discovered that there is no 'right' way to see the world. Whilst most of us think that the way we see things is the way that they actually are, we are in fact operating from our own inner map of the world, our inner perception. Although a map can guide us *through* the territory, it is only a representation – my inner world is a *representation* of the external world, but it is *not* the external world.

I used to go to the local Italian delicatessen to buy a slab of pizza. I had always disliked the crusty bits, but being brought up to be polite I accepted whichever piece of the pizza I was given. Then, one day, the man in front of me asked for five slices and I heard him ask, "Could I have all crusty pieces please. They are my favourite." This was a revelation to me, and gave me permission to ask for the middle pieces. My perception had changed: rather than it feeling selfish to ask for the pieces I liked, now I could see that it could be generous by leaving the crusty pieces for the people who really loved them!

My second therapy training was a Diploma in Professional Counselling. This taught me to work with individual clients. When, after several years, a couple came for therapy, it became clear that giving therapy to two people brings additional complexities. I decided to attend a weekend workshop on working with relationships. On the second day the facilitator took me to one side and said, "You have a talent for this couples work. Might you be interested in doing more? There is a two-year training." I signed up almost straightaway. So, in 1997, I began training as a couples therapist at the Maudsley Hospital with Dr Michael Crowe and Jane Ridley. We were taught the 'behavioural-systemic' method. In the mornings we would cover theory and in the afternoons we would have a clinic, where clients came for therapy sessions with us trainees. A new world of psychotherapy was opening up to me, and I was loving it – and beginning to learn a lot about my own relationship patterns.

Around that time I came across the work of David Schnarch. In my family of origin, we lived in a permanent state of fusion, with everyone tiptoeing around to 'keep Dad happy'. Since that was all I knew, that was what I had taken into my early relationships. I thought that it was my job to keep the other person happy, and their job to keep me happy. Poor R, my first husband! Schnarch, and his work on emotional fusion, helped me to profoundly re-evaluate my understanding of what love is. His work introduced me to the idea that when we sign up for a relationship we hope that the other will operate from the best in themselves, and that if *I* am to be in integrity in my relationship, then it is my responsibility to bring my optimum self where *I* can. I did not do this in my early relationships.

Schnarch also helped me to work out my approach to sex. I now believe that each person is responsible for their own sexual arousal, orgasm, and release. In other words, I have a responsibility to work on my receptivity, to learn how to arouse myself, and to be able to deal with my sexual frustration by masturbation. It is not my partner's job to deal with, and satisfy, all my sexual tensions. On the other hand, if I am going to be a good partner in a relationship, I have a responsibility to work on any blocks to my ability to become aroused (and orgasmic), and my partner has a right to expect some sexual and intimate contact in our relationship, and vice versa. How that manifests will be different in every partnership, but each person has a right to expect sexual contact in their intimate relationship, unless or until they have both agreed that that is not a key part in their partnership.

In 2001, William introduced me to the Pesso Boyden System Psychomotor (PBSP) approach. I fell into an enduring love with the work.

Having already received about twelve years of excellent therapy, I was shocked to find that I was working on many of the same issues that I had already covered in previous therapy. At first this was disappointing, but I recognised the deeper healing that was happening through PBSP. In my 'talking' therapy, we had worked on issues on the psychological level, but in the PBSP structures I found that there were memories and traumas that had been stored *in my body* which needed to be released. This time, when I worked on my old issues with PBSP, the issues (by and large) went away, never to return.

I'm very fortunate, my work is enormously satisfying. Whether it is working with an individual with a sexual issue, with a couple who are struggling to be happy together, or with one of the members of my experiential groups, I love watching people grow and develop. I get inspired by authenticity and honesty, and quite often feel full, even overwhelmed with love. I respect people's dedication to their own growth, and get great pleasure when I hear about the beneficial shifts that people make. These may be small and subtle, or larger and more obvious, but they are often profound changes that help people to deal with their lives, as they make the journey to be more fully who they truly are. It helps me to stay on track, and to be more fully who I am, too.

Beyond All That

We don't do touchy-feely, you and I...
We're sharp and clever, resourceful people.
But when, in the middle of the night,
I turn to find you there — still there —
despite my dreams and the dread of waking.
I reach out to touch you, and the fear melts away,
and I am thankful beyond measure.

We don't do religion, you and I...
We like to think we're beyond all that:
the rules, the hypocrisies, the tired old ceremonies.
But when I find you, sitting alone,
bathed in quiet at the end of the day,
the last of the sunlight tumbling over you,
I want to say, I believe in you —
that you are my homing, and my haven.

We don't do demonstrative, you and I...
We don't feel the need to go over the top.
We don't send flowers. We don't hire planes
to write "I love you" across the busy sky...
But when I know that you are hurting,
when the world's a cruel and hollow place,
there's a part of me that wants to shout
across the roof-tops that you are mine,
and that I will love you come what may —
what e'er befall us — whatever comes.

William Ayot

Appendix 1
Glossary of terms

Antidote: In PBSP the antidote is a symbolic corrective experience, which is a precisely-fitting alternative to the client's real history. The purpose of the antidote is to counteract the toxic effects of the client's original history[1]. It is created using (symbolic) Ideal Figures who are in the right kinship relationship to the client, who provide the fitting interactive experience to the client at the right age (see Right Kinship Relationship and at the Right Age). For example, if the original parents were violent and shouted at each other, then the Ideal Parents would be kind and calm; if the original parents lacked boundaries then the Ideal Parents would be appropriately firm.

Click of Closure: A term used in PBSP. Every time we make things complete there is a 'click of closure'; an internal 'pleasure pop' which is our innate reward system.

Counter-shape: A PBSP term used in the context of 'shape and counter-shape'. If the *hand* is a 'shape' then a closely-fitting leather *glove* that follows the contours of the hand would be the 'counter-shape', the perfect match. The client's *need* may be the shape, and the counter-shape is the precisely-fitting, wished for, *satisfaction* of that need. The client's *action* may be the shape, and there will be a satisfying *response* to that action (the counter-shape).

Couple structure: In PBSP this is where a couple have two independent structures (client sessions) that run parallel to each other, and start within a short time of each other. One structure begins, and will continue for approximately ten minutes, then that structure is paused. The structure for the second person is then started, and runs for ten to fifteen minutes, and is then paused. The total time for the couple structure is just under two hours. It offers couples an opportunity to explore issues that have been causing problems between them and to see how their histories have interwoven to create those issues.

Differentiation: Murray Bowen[2] referred to differentiation as the process of freeing yourself from other people's feelings and thoughts, so that you can define yourself whilst staying emotionally connected to the other person. David Schnarch defines it as "your ability to keep your emotional balance while interacting in important relationships."[3] It is a healthy separateness.

Ego: In PBSP the ego is the psychological boundary of a person (the skin of the soul). The ego is constructed through interactions with significant others, and is conditioned through historical and cultural events. The ego 'decides' what to let in and what to put out, discriminating between: self and other, reality and fantasy, dream and awake, etc.[4] The combination of the soul and the ego comprises the self,[5] and it is optimal when the ego fits the soul closely, like a well-made suit fits a body; not too tight, not too loose, just right. This is achieved by parents who are able to 'counter-shape' the soul of their child. (see Counter-shape).

Ego too strong: If the ego is too strong it stops the soul from being expressed. Examples would be someone who is obsessive-compulsive, or who has no conscious feelings, just thoughts. With a 'too strong' ego, the soul impulse comes out but it doesn't reach the border of expression, because the ego is too big and restrictive.

Ego too fragile: If the ego is too fragile, then emotions are popping out all over the place; the person has little or no control over his or her actions and 'spills into the universe', having no shape.

Ego-wrap: In PBSP this term describes the act of applying consciousness, names, acceptance, and place on a portion of the soul/self when it makes an appearance in a structure. This is achieved by a Witness Figure, an Ideal Figure, or a Permission Giving Figure, etc.[6]

Emotional Fusion: A term used first by Murray Bowen,[7] and later by David Schnarch[8] to describe the situation where one partner is dependent upon the other for their emotional balance. They are unable to appropriately separate their feelings from others, and become fused with their partner's emotions, inappropriately absorbing the anxieties and worries of their partner, and becoming debilitated. It is also known as co-dependence.

Figures in the air: In PBSP sometimes Ideal Figures will be 'in the air', i.e. in the imagination, or given a place in the room, but without an object or a person enrolled as that Figure to materially represent it.

Films: In PBSP a film or a movie is the scene created, using objects, to fill Holes in Roles. The therapist creates a mini 'theatrical event', using objects to represent people, much in the way that a child will play with dolls. The client watches this scene as an 'outside observer'. It is as if they are seeing a short film on TV, but with characters from their own life. For example, Sheila in Chapter 4 part 2 saw her real father with his 'Ideal Wife'. The therapist, by creating a believable 'film' of that possibility, enabled her to step out of that role. Sheila had the 'click of closure' (see above), of seeing her real father's satisfaction, without *her* having to do anything. Because her father had the wife he needed, and it wasn't her who was doing that for him, she no longer had to 'step in' and rescue him. Also known as movies. (see Holes in Roles).

Holes in Roles: In PBSP filling Holes in Roles means that the client as a child has (involuntarily and often unconsciously) created a fantasy of being the helper to someone, by stepping in to fulfil a role that has been missing for that person. This impulse is provoked where there is a gap[9] or injustice in the network of family roles and relationships, and a child's compassion has been awakened too early and before their basic needs have been met. For example, if the mother died, then the child may unconsciously make a movie in their mind where they imagine themselves filling the role of a wife for their father. They may make another movie where they fill the role of a mother for each of their siblings. Unconscious movies where they are the healer can even be done for the cultural system, the religious system, and also for characters from fairy stories or historical stories. Children can, in their fantasy, go back through time and space to fill a hole in an earlier generation. A consequence of filling holes in roles is a sense of omnipotence, which occurs outside the client's awareness. The goal in PBSP is to bring these holes (that the client has unconsciously filled) to a conscious level, so that they can be worked out on a symbolic level[10]. This is done by having an appropriate other person filling the hole in a completely believable, effective and satisfying way. This enables the client to 'hand the role back over', which brings great relief, and clients often feel as if a burden has been lifted. A Magical Marriage is a particular type of hole in role, which occurs where the child has filled the role of a partner to one of their parents. (see Films, Magical Marriage, Omnipotence)

Ideal Father; Ideal Mother: In PBSP an Ideal Father – or Ideal Mother – is the wished for, missing father – or mother – with attributes that were longed for in one's childhood. The role is played by a group member.[11]

Ideal Figures: In PBSP Ideal Figures are constructed to match the needs of a client, so that those needs that were not met in childhood can be symbolically experienced and satisfied[12]. For example, if the client's real father was aggressive, the Ideal Father will be kind, if their real father was too soft, the Ideal Father will hold appropriate boundaries and be able to be firm. This is done using the shape – counter-shape concept. (see Counter-shape, Ideal Father).

Magical Marriage: In PBSP this happens when a child feels compassion for their parent, and makes a spontaneous unconscious movie or fantasy, where they themselves fill a role, in this case giving their parent what a partner should have given. This inappropriate relationship is created out of their conscious awareness, and can have lifelong consequences. A Magical Marriage is one type of 'hole in role' (see Holes in Roles). In PBSP we create a 'counter-movie' by filling the role of partner with another person, so that the client can feel 'released from the partnering responsibility and burden'[13].

Micro-tracking: In PBSP, micro-tracking is when the therapist focuses on the client's present consciousness. This includes paying attention to the client's face and the mercurial micro-shifts of expression showing there, while also attending to the client's posture, actions, gestures, words and tone of voice. This enables the therapist to observe the affective states, emotional expressions, behaviours and thoughts of the client. The therapist then makes these observations available to the client using a Witness figure to name (out loud) this information about the client's emotions, at the very moments they are occurring, accompanied by the exact context that the client was talking about in that moment. We use Voice figures to play back to the client his or her (more stifling and restricting) thoughts about themselves, the world, and how to interact with it, on the assumption that this 'map' of 'reality' has been built on the basis of prior experiences in the client's history. Both elements enrich the client's pilot.[14] (see Pilot, Witness). The structure and architecture of the client's issues is thus represented in minute detail, and this not only supports consciousness, but also awakens conscious memories of those *events* which provided the underlying foundation for present emotions, thoughts and life-strategies. Seeing the 'here and now' awakens the 'there and then' of the client, who will begin to realise where issues may have arisen.

Movies: (See films).

NLP: Neuro-Linguistic Programming is a method of personal development, communication and psychotherapy that was created by Richard Bandler and John Grinder in the 1970s. From studying the structure of an individual's everyday experience in detail, particularly focusing on people who were considered exceptional in their field, NLP developed: i) a set of presuppositions (guiding principles and attitudes); ii) a methodology for modelling (what to observe and how to 'frame' that); iii) a system of coding (how to frame a detailed description); iv) a series of models (different ways of understanding) and v) a trail of techniques (things to do).[15]

Non-genital sensate focus (or sensate touching): A set of exercises which aims to enhance the experience and satisfaction of sexual contact. In stage 1: sexual penetration is banned, and the genitals and breasts are 'out of bounds' and cannot be touched. The couple agree to two or three sessions of sensuous touching a week. Stage 2: the touching includes the genitals but penetration and orgasm are still banned. Stage 3: everything is reintroduced, including sexual intercourse. Used with Frank and Maxine in Chapter 2.

One and only: The one and only is where there is absolutely 'no other'. That is, there is no interactive object; no-one else to rely on. The person who takes the position of the one and only is 'All-That-There-Is', and is in a God-like position of omnipotence. (see Omnipotence).

Omnipotence: In PBSP we see this in a few different situations. For example, omnipotence may be the result of a lack of appropriate limits, so that energies remain unbounded (e.g. sexual energy or aggressive energy). Trauma (where the boundary of the self has been violated and broken) can lead to omnipotent vulnerability or rage. Another type of omnipotence occurs when we have filled holes in roles (and we become the omnipotent caretaker for others; we are the only one who can really look after them properly). A lack of parenting (or ego-constructing figures) during important developmental stages[16] can leave us with the feeling of unlimited and unstoppable power or openness. Clients may indicate omnipotence by saying, *No one can do it but me*, or *my needs and capacities are infinite, and cannot be satisfied by another* or *this won't work for me – nothing will ever work for me – I am too damaged for any therapy to succeed*. Omnipotence is connected to being the 'one and only' that can do it. (see Ego, Holes in Roles, One and Only, and Trauma).

PBSP: Created in 1961 by Albert Pesso and Diane Boyden-Pesso, Pesso Boyden System Psychotherapy (PBSP) is a highly advanced therapeutic system for emotional re-education or re-programming. PBSP heals past emotional deficits using unique processes called Structures and Micro-tracking that help clients to identify emotional deficits and create 'new memories'. These 'new memories' provide symbolic fulfilment of the basic developmental needs of place, nurture, support, protection and limits. With the inclusion of Holes in Roles, therapists learn how to provide a highly effective and streamlined approach to reducing resistance, negative transference, and somatic overload. Many aspects of PBSP theories and techniques have close parallels in recent neuroscience findings about mirror neurons, empathy, morality, and the impact of language on the theory of mind.[17]

Pilot: In PBSP the Pilot is the highest order of consciousness. Being the primary face of the ego, the Pilot organises the ego functions[18]. The Pilot observes everything, and can also be conscious of itself, has the overview, makes decisions, and takes responsibility.

Placeholders: In PBSP these are objects that are used in a structure to represent a person, or a place that has been spoken about by the client. The Placeholder stands for the 'filing cabinet' of all the memories, associations, projections, needs and hopes that the client connects to that particular person, both positive and negative.

Principles: In PBSP Principles are used when a client mentions a person and their reactions to them, and discovers that they have subconsciously projected emotional associations that originated from experiences with other people, often their primary caregivers early in life[19]. This linkage is represented by a little object or piece of paper representing that Principle, which is put on the Placeholder. This process is used in conjunction with Ideal Parents and Reversals Techniques, which provide new positive memories to replace the old memories that accounted for the negative (or positive) transference and projection. For example, the client might have the Principle of the Real Mother (and her aggression) sitting on his partner, because he experienced violence at the hands of his real mother when he was a child. In the structure, after an antidote of a non-violent Ideal Mother, the Principle of his Real Mother (and her aggression) will be taken off the (Placeholder for the) partner, and put onto (a Placeholder for) the real mother. Thus the partner is no longer carrying the 'loading' from history – the expectation that they will be aggressive.

Psychosexual therapy: Also known as psychosexual counselling, this is a service offered by specially trained psychotherapists and counsellors, who have the skills to work with a wide variety of sexual issues.

Reversals: A PBSP technique where the therapist helps the client to create a new memory that is a reversal of the challenging or traumatic experience from the past. Often a first step is the simple negation of the historical facts (an Ideal Parent would not have done what the real parent did, or would have done what the real parent failed to do). Later in the structure the Ideal Parent figure can be elaborated upon, to do things that the client longed for when they were a child.

Right kinship relationship and at the right age: In PBSP the healing interactions must symbolically happen in the hypothetical past at the *right age* for the client (i.e. the same age that the original lack or wounding happened) and with the *correct kinship relationship*. If a mother neglected her child, then the reversal would be with a nurturing Ideal Mother, who might say to the client: *If I had been your Ideal Mother when you were five-years-old, I would have been attentive, and I would have nourished you in just the way you needed.*

Shape: (see Counter-shape).

Soul: The PBSP definition is that the soul is all that you are, and all of your potential; it is your true self. It is not a thing, it is the pure process of endlessly becoming, pushing forward to survive in the present and thrive in the future. Our task in life is to fulfil our soul potential. The outer membrane that fits around the soul is called the ego, and this is formed through interactions, a process known in PBSP as Ego-wrapping. The soul lives in the body and expresses itself through the body. (see Ego, Ego-wrap, True Self).

Symbolic: In PBSP we help clients to understand the difference between literal and symbolic. For example, if we think about the need for nurture, a baby is literally fed with his mother's milk, and while he is fed, he is looking at his mother, who looks back with love and approval, so the baby is simultaneously fed by the literal milk, and symbolically nourished by the mother's love. Having understood the difference between reality and symbolic, on an intellectual level *and* on an emotional level, people can consciously create and manipulate their symbolic world. The satisfaction that is felt from adjusting the *symbolic* world is a *real, truly felt, literal* satisfaction, which creates biological changes. In the symbolic reality, the Ideal Parents can say, 'I would have been there for you always,' and the client experiences this, although the literal contact with the role-player ends after the de-roling.

Structure: The name for a PBSP client session. These are designed to help clients review past, life-determining situation(s) in a completely accepting atmosphere, called the 'possibility sphere'. The therapist then helps the client construct an antidote to the original event with appropriate Ideal Kinship Figures, in interactions that support and confirm gene-based expectations of success in surviving and thriving. This is achieved with the help of new, healing, memory-building symbolic events which take place in the therapy room and are seen with the client's *real* eyes and felt in the client's *real* body. They are then placed, with the aid of the *mind*'s eye and the *mind*'s body, in the appropriate storage space in the brain where real old memories are kept and can later be accessed. The client constructs the kinds of interactions they seek. The end result is a hopeful, more optimistic person with an ego-structure more able to regulate and control both the inner and outer domains.[20]

Trauma: PBSP defines trauma as *too much (unwanted) coming in*. This happens when the skin has literally been penetrated (for example, if one is attacked by a knife, and also in medical interventions such as surgery). Trauma also occurs when the body boundaries are violated by violence or sexual abuse, or if one is psychologically and verbally attacked (which penetrates the skin of the ego, and the sense of the self). A trauma is a threat which is more powerful than the client's ability to hold it off and/or heal the experience with his or her normal psychological capacities. Traumatic experiences are usually experienced as overwhelming and flooding, and result in an alternative psycho-physiological state. Thus, they are not stored in the usual ways, often making it hard to process the trauma verbally. Because PBSP is a body-based therapy, it can be very valuable in the treatment of trauma. People who've been traumatised may experience intrusive memories and hyper-vigilance to certain stimuli. Please note, PBSP makes a distinction between something that in common language is described as traumatic (e.g. neglect, where the basic needs are not being met – which is defined in PBSP as a deficit, so there is *too little coming in*), and a *trauma* which is an intrusion, where there is *too much coming in*.

True Self: In PBSP this refers to a person's human potential. What a person would become under ideal physical, emotional, and societal circumstances. The True Self constantly reacts to the events in a person's life, although the person may not be consciously aware of this reaction.[21] (see Soul)

Unconscious: Out of our awareness, so that we have no idea that this has happened.

Voice: In PBSP a Voice is a conclusion, or an assumption, or a way of being, learned from experience based on our history. A Voice summarises a conclusion from our experience about how the world is and how to best manoeuvre in it, e.g. *parents are not reliable*, or *better not rely on anybody*. The Voices in PBSP are not benign and caring like the Witness Figure, but are generally negative or pessimistic. They are used to announce back to clients in a declarative or imperative way the unhelpful attitudes, strategies, and unsupportive values that clients have accumulated through life experience, often responded to as if they were hypnotic suggestions and 'carved in stone'.[22] Hearing these Voices from the outside helps clients learn that these are not absolute truths, and that they can be questioned and changed.

Witness: In PBSP this is a symbolic, benign and compassionate figure that appears in every structure. It supports the Pilot. Although witnessing is also a function of Ideal Parents, since it supports the development of consciousness, the Witness Figure is in the present and sees and responds to the client's emotional states and nuances of mood, naming them and putting them in context, giving acknowledgement, licence to exist, dimensions, and blessing.[23]

Appendix 2

The kind of sessions
that Juliet Grayson and her team offer

One-to-one therapy, groups, and intensives

One-to-One

Juliet Grayson has a private practice in South Wales where she
sees clients. Sessions last between one hour, for people who live
locally, and anything up to five hours for those travelling a long
way. She specialises in relationship issues, sexual problems and
people who are facing a life-limiting/terminal diagnosis. Juliet
offers Pesso Boyden in one-to-one sessions as well as in groups.

'Couples in Calamity' sessions

These sessions are designed for couples who want an intensive
private session with a therapist. Generally, they last for seven
hours over two days – Juliet meets with the couple for three
and a half hours on one afternoon, the couple stays locally, and
then the three of them meet again for three and a half hours the
following morning. Sometimes there will be a follow up session,
by agreement, after a few weeks or months.

Juliet's team across the UK

Juliet has a team of therapists in different parts of the UK who
can work with a wide range of issues, including one-to-one
sessions, couple therapy, Pesso Boyden therapy and psychosexual
therapy. Some of these are able to offer 'couples in calamity' and
intensive sessions.

Pesso Boyden System Psychomotor groups

One-day workshops

Occasionally Juliet runs one-day workshops. Participants, who have never met each other before, arrive, have a cup of tea, and mingle. Then the workshop commences. Juliet often begins with a short lecture to introduce PBSP, and then she runs four structures (client sessions). There is a closing round where everyone reflects on what they are taking from the day, before everyone leaves. It is interesting to watch how quickly people open up. It seems that the PBSP method and techniques really help trust – and a sense of safety – to build for the participants.

PBSP closed experiential groups

Most of Juliet's PBSP work is done in closed, ongoing, experiential groups. This means that the same people gather each time, usually meeting for a total of eight days over a year, in four blocks each lasting two days[24]. Typically, there will be between ten and fourteen people participating in these ongoing groups. The group has time to get to know each other and their issues, and often this enables the work to deepen. Some people will continue on to the next year, and on occasions, the whole group has decided that they would like to do a second, third or even a fourth year together. Juliet runs these PBSP personal development groups in different locations across the UK. Each group 'opens' once a year to take in new members (subject to space).

Residential four-day Pesso Boyden group 'Deep-Dive' intensives

Twice a year Juliet runs a four-day residential group, for between eleven and fourteen people; during the four days, each person has one structure. The group process develops, and the bond between group members deepens. The warmth and closeness in these residential workshops can be very enriching and touching.

Couples attending my PBSP groups

For a couple, working in a PBSP group can be profoundly informative and helpful. Even where there are difficulties and struggles, they can work well. Maybe the couple had a row on the way to the workshop and are feeling upset or angry with each other when they arrive. Once one person has a structure, the authenticity, honesty and vulnerability shown will generally elicit compassion from their partner. This is profoundly healing to the couple. Understanding the root of a partner's issues often brings a new quality of tolerance to the relationship. Another option is to have a 'couple structure', where both people are involved in structures at the same time. These can be beneficial for working on issues that have arisen *between* the partners. Usually couples leave feeling closer, and more whole than when they arrived.

Some of the benefits of witnessing other people's structures

Juliet encourages group members to engage in vicarious healing. During a structure Juliet invites each person, if the issue resonates with them, to imagine that the Ideal Parents (or whatever figures have been enrolled) are speaking to them. They can change the words slightly in their inner ear, so they hear the words that *they* need. This can in itself be profound, and people often express gratitude for the healing they received when someone else was working.

Being in a group is a good way to recognise those issues that we may not been aware of, or have denied. As we observe other people's structures, we may find we are deeply moved by one sentence, or one section. This often provides a clue, that in relation to this part of our history, our inner world was not as quiet and 'sorted' as we had thought.

Courses for people who want to work directly on their relationships

Juliet Grayson and her husband, William Ayot, occasionally run workshops for couples and individuals who want help with their relationships. Two of their workshops, *The Real Deal* and *The Odd Couple,* have proved very popular.

Courses for therapists who work one-to-one and want to work with couples

Juliet Grayson (and her team of trainers) run a six-module workshop (twelve days in total) teaching the different aspects of working with couples. The different modules are *The Fundamentals of Working with Couples, Communication and Difference, Dealing with Affairs, Couples In Conflict, Sex Arousal and Ageing,* and *Meeting Their Partner's Developmental Needs.* You will find further information about these courses on her website: www.therapyandcounselling.co.uk

Training to become a Pesso Boyden System Psychomotor therapist

This is a three-year, part-time training, covering both theory and practice. People may also join just for the first year. For more information please see www.PessoBoydenTrainingUK.com

For further information:

www.therapyandcounselling.co.uk
www.landscapesoftheheart.co.uk
www.sexuallyinappropriatebehaviour.org

Please follow Juliet Grayson on Twitter:
@HelpingYouBeYou and also @CounsellorsCPD

www.facebook.com/JulietGraysonRelationships

Appendix 3
How to find a therapist

As a human being, I understand why it takes people so long to attend therapy – especially couples, where both parties have to be willing. But as a couples therapist I would love to get the message across that couple therapy is not so difficult. The longer people leave the problem, the more entrenched their habits and negative beliefs about one another will become. In my experience, couples have usually been having problems for at least two years, and often more, before they come for therapy or counselling. If there is also a sexual component to the problem, then generally it will be three to five years before they come for therapy. Yet it would have been so much quicker to resolve it if they had come within the first year of the problem arising! So this book is partially a call to couples who are struggling, to say, "Come for therapy. It can really help! And come soon – don't wait until it is almost too late."

When looking for a therapist, a personal recommendation is always a good start. Ask friends, as well as friends of friends. I recommend speaking to a few therapists on the phone, and having a preliminary session with two or three therapists. See who you click with. Who could you open up with? Who do you trust? You don't necessarily need to like them, but you should feel that you can work with your chosen therapist.

If it is a relationship issue, then please check out the level of professional training that the therapist has had in this area (and that they have had some!). Working with two people may seem similar to one-to-one therapy, but it is surprisingly different. The skills a one-to-one therapist has will all be useful and relevant, but extra expertise is needed. Generally, it is recognised that working with two people is more than twice as complex, and you need to be sure that your therapist is familiar and comfortable with this.

If it is a sexual issue then, again, check that the therapist has had specialist training to deal with sexual problems. Sometimes the sexual issue is primarily a relationship problem – in which case a relationship therapist is fine. But if you need specialist psychosexual help, then someone who is *not* trained in this way will be guessing and fumbling in the dark. You wouldn't go to a motorbike mechanic to mend your car. If there is not a psychosexual therapist in your area, then I recommend you start by talking to the relationship therapist who is closest. Check that they will be honest if they feel that your issue is more complex than they are currently able to work with. You want to know that, if needed, they will refer you on. Some therapists feel like they are letting their clients down and worry that the client will feel rejected if they pass them on, but it can be the wisest choice, saving you both time and money.

If you are attracted to Pesso Boyden therapy, which is the most effective method that I have come across, then you may need to travel. As yet, there are not a huge number of therapists who are trained to work in this way in the UK.

If a personal recommendation is not forthcoming, then check out these websites:

www.PessoBoydenTrainingUK.com
The Pesso Boyden System Psychomotor website will put you in touch with PBSP certified practitioners in the UK. At present there are a small number. There is also information here about how to train as a PBSP therapist.

www.pessoboydenuk.org

This website gives you a list of PBSP workshops.

www.psychotherapy.org.uk

The United Kingdom Council for Psychotherapy website is good for finding one-to-one therapists.

www.cosrt.org.uk

The College of Sex and Relationship Therapists website has both sexual and relationship therapists.

www.nlptca.com

The Neurolinguistic Psychotherapy and Counselling Association will connect you with a therapist who specialises in NLP.

www.pbsp.com

There are a lot of PBSP resources on the co-founders', Al Pesso and Diane Boyden-Pesso, website. This page has many unpublished articles http://pbsp.com/theory-techniques/books/unpublished-manuscripts-by-al-pesso-and-diane-boyden-pesso/

To contact Juliet Grayson, or for a referral (for counselling) to a member of her team, contact:
Juliet@therapyandcounselling.co.uk or
visit her website: **www.therapyandcounselling.co.uk**

Appendix 4
The importance of having a medical check for sexual problems

I could not allow the book to be published without acknowledging the importance of including a medical assessment when there is a sexual problem. Eliminating a medical problem before commencing therapy is vital. Obviously, if the cause is physical then that should be treated by doctors. Occasionally there is both a medical and a psychological element, in which case combining medical treatment and psychotherapy is very beneficial. For example, when a man or a woman has a clinically low level of testosterone and does not feel like sex, then there is little point in spending weeks working therapeutically on their desire issues. It is better for the medical professional to treat the medical issue with suitable medication (i.e. with testosterone) and normalise those levels within the body. However, often there is something in the relationship that needs improving too – and therapeutic work will be essential, alongside the use of medication.

I remember the woman who told me about how she had suffered for decades with a back problem. Doctors had found no cause. She concluded that was due to neglect and abuse in her childhood and a lack of support in her youth, and spent many years in therapy. Eventually, she trained as a Jungian analyst. Every morning, for thirty years, she spent an hour noting her dreams and writing a journal. Her back pain continued. Finally, now in her 60s, she was diagnosed as having one leg shorter than the other. She put a very thick foam pad inside one shoe, and the pain went within a few days. The psychological work she had done had been beneficial in her life, but did not help her back pain. She had a physical problem that needed a physical solution.

Another example was a man who found his pornography use escalating, and was concerned that he was a sex addict or a potential sex offender. Blood test results indicated a clinically low testosterone level of 5.8 nmol/L. After six months of using testosterone gel to increase his testosterone levels, he found that his desire to use pornography fell away, and his pornography use completely stopped. The underlying problem was his lack of arousal and he had found (what he thought of as) a solution – the use of porn. He didn't even need therapy alongside the testosterone treatment.

A third client had panic attacks and again found therapy was not helping. Someone suggested she take magnesium – so she saw a nutritionist, started on a programme of magnesium and immediately her symptoms improved. She has not had a problem with panic attacks since then. So while therapy can be invaluable and life-changing, if there is an underlying medical problem, it is essential that that problem is addressed. Please note, if you organise blood tests in search of a cause for panic attacks, check red blood cell magnesium, as it is a more useful marker than serum magnesium, which is the standard medical text but which would rarely ever show any imbalance.

If the idea of sending clients to have blood tests is daunting for a therapist, bear in mind what Trevor Shelley said when addressing a group of psychosexual therapists in Hampshire:

> "It would, of course, be unreasonable to expect any non-medically qualified therapist to *deal* with these medical problems but it *is* reasonable to expect that they will be competent enough to recognise them and to ensure that action by an appropriate medical expert is then brought into play."[25]

I will always involve the GP where there is an issue of a loss of sexual drive, or a loss of arousal (for a man who has difficulty getting an erection, or for a woman who has a lack of lubrication) or pain. Usually the client gets the following blood tests checked (these tests are written up in a paper[26] I co-wrote):

Fasting Glucose: To check for diabetes. Almost 50% of diabetic clients have sexual functioning difficulties. Problems with arousal (erectile problems and vaginal dryness) are symptoms of poorly-managed diabetes. This blood test should be taken when the patient has had no food for fourteen hours.

Lipid Ratio: To check for vascular disease (which can cause heart disease and circulatory disease). Arousal problems indicate the need for this test. Check if the client can walk without pain for a mile. If this causes pain in their legs, it may be due to intermittent claudication, which is the narrowing of blood vessels to the legs, and can be an early warning sign of cardiovascular disease. If you think about it, the blood vessels to the genitals are thinner than those to the heart and so they fur up sooner. Research shows that arousal problems can be an early indicator of heart problems, which may occur some three to five years later.[27]

Prolactin: To check for a brain tumour. This should be a resting test, i.e. the client arrives at least 20 minutes before the blood sample is taken. Please note that elevated prolactin levels could also be due to stress, or a clash with other medication.

Testosterone: To check for problems of low testosterone (in both men and women). This can cause desire disorders, arousal disorders (poor quality erection, vaginal dryness, loss of pleasure or sensation), pain and fatigue disorders. Often the client feels like their 'get up and go' has 'got up and gone'. This blood test should be taken before 10.00am.

Sex Hormone Binding Globulin (SHBG): Elevated levels may indicate less available testosterone since SHBG binds to testosterone.

Thyroid Stimulating Hormone (TSH): To check for thyroid problems. Low levels may result in tiredness and loss of sexual interest (and other issues).

Full Blood Count (FBC): To check for anaemia, which may result in tiredness and loss of sexual interest (and other issues).

Liver function test (LFT): To check how well the liver is working. It is wise to check liver function especially if the client reports excessive alcohol intake (e.g. twice the recommended allowance).

Oestrogen (women only): To check for menopausal changes affecting physical arousal. A decrease in oestrogen levels during the menopause can cause vaginal tissues to become thin and less elastic (vaginal atrophy) causing pain.

Prostate-specific antigen (PSA) (men only): To check for an enlarged or inflamed prostate, or a urinary tract infection.

Results of the above: Most of these blood tests and levels are standardised and well documented. I always ask the client to bring me a printout of their results (the doctor's receptionist will happily supply these to the patient) so that even if the results are normal, I can check if they are in the mid-range, or at the low or high end of 'normal'. If you are a therapist, I recommend finding a suitably trained supervisor (or medically trained person) who can help with double checking blood test results – although generally if a problem is highlighted the GP will act on it. However, testosterone levels are an exception. Where the testosterone levels are below 12 nmol/L for a man, then treatment with testosterone replacement should be considered. If they are slightly higher but there are other symptoms (such as lack of energy, decrease in strength, sex drive, endurance, or work performance, sadness, grumpiness, erections that are not as hard, or falling asleep after dinner) then testosterone supplementation might still be advised.

Historically, in the UK, no normative study for investigation of female testosterone level has ever been carried out and therefore in some parts of the country, women can have a testosterone level of 0 and this still be assessed as normal! Colleagues and I think that this is due to the fact that researchers have used an average of womens' levels rather than normative study. For a woman whose testosterone levels are below 1.5 nmol/L it is wise to consider supplementation. Blood test results alone are not conclusive, but should be taken into account with other physical symptoms such as lack of drive and desire, tiredness, low mood, irritability, poor concentration, dry eyes and night sweats. Please note that treatment for this may not be available on the NHS, and clients may need to see a private doctor or endocrinologist for advice.

Appendix 5

Where to go for help if you have sexually inappropriate thoughts

StopSO: Specialist Treatment Organisation for the Prevention of Sexual Offending

StopSO UK is a not-for-profit organisation that is working to stop sexual offending through therapy.

Set up by Juliet Grayson and a team of colleagues, StopSO has created a nationwide network of psychotherapists, psychologists and counsellors. These people are trained to work with anyone who is worried about their sexual behaviour, who feels that they may be at risk of committing a sexual offence, or re-offending. This may include: voyeurism, exhibitionism, looking at illegal images (e.g. bestiality or child abuse images), and contact offending with adults or children, etc. StopSO also offers therapy for the families of those who have committed a sexual offence.

Providing this service is seen as a safeguarding issue to protect all members of society from the devastating consequences of sexual offending. All the clients contacting StopSO are motivated, and are asking for help to stop their inappropriate sexual behaviour.

Of the clients contacting StopSO[28], 83% are self-referred, and 34% have not yet come to the attention of the police or social services. Many of these are non-offending paedophiles, who have never broken the law. They have never looked at child abuse images, nor acted on their urges in any other way. They are motivated, and asking for help. By providing this help in the community, StopSO is not only reducing sexual re-offending, but is also helping to stop the *first* sexual offence.

StopSO provides specialist training workshops all over the UK, so that counsellors, psychotherapists, psychologists and other professionals can gain the necessary skills to work with this client group. StopSO also provides: safeguarding training to schools and agencies, support to employers who have had to deal with the aftermath of an employee being arrested for a sexual offence, an online support group for the families of sexual offenders, specialist supervision for any therapist who is working with this client group and an online support group for professionals working in this field.

There is an anonymous research questionnaire on the StopSO website. Please ask anyone struggling with inappropriate sexual behaviour to fill it in.

Therapists can apply to join the StopSO register: see the criteria on the website.

Clients can access this private sector service via the website, email, or telephone.

Our aim is to prevent damage and protect society.

www.stopso.org.uk
Telephone: **07473 299883**
Email: **info@stopso.org.uk**

Appendix 6
Select Bibliography

Ayot, W. (2003). *Small things that matter*. London, UK: The Well.

Ayot, W. (2014). *The inheritance*. Chepstow, UK: Sleeping Mountain Press.

Ayot, W. (2014). *E-mail from the soul: new and selected leadership poems*. Somerset, UK: Sleeping Mountain Press.

Ayot, W. (2015) *Re-enchanting the Forest: Meaningful Ritual in a Secular World*. Bristol, UK: Vala

Crowe, M., & Ridley, J. (2008). *Therapy with Couples: A Behavioural-Systems Approach To Couple Relationship And Sexual Problems*. Chichester, UK: John Wiley & Sons.

Gottman, J. (2005). *Making Marriage Work (Live)*. Better Life Media Audio Inc [Audio book].

Grayson, J. (2014). Back to the root. Healing potential sexual offenders' childhood trauma with Pesso Boyden System Psychomotor. In Hudson-Allez (Ed), *Sexual Diversity and Sexual Offending: Research, Assessment, and Clinical Treatment in Psychosexual Therapy* (pp. 251-273). London, UK: Karnac Books.

Grayson, J. (2015). Unravelling Complexities, tidying up our intimate relationships. In Lowe (Ed), *The PPD Learning NLP practice group book: The special guest sessions*. UK: Maxfield Press

Hendrix, H. (1988). *Getting the love you want: A guide for couples*. New York: H. Holt.

Hillman, J. (1996). *The soul's code: In search of character and calling.* New York: Random House.

Horacek, J., Pesso, A., Tintera, J., Vancura, M., Luck, L., Kobrle, L., Dockery, C. (2005). The effect of two sessions of PBSP Psychotherapy on brain activation in response to trauma-related stimuli: the pilot fMRI study in traumatized persons. *Psychiatrie (Czech Journal), 3.*

Hudson-Allez, G. (2011). *Infant losses, adult searches: A neural and developmental perspective on psychopathology and sexual offending.* London, UK: Karnac. Kindle.

Kerr, M., & Bowen, M. (1988). *Family Evaluation: An Approach Based on Bowen Theory.* London, UK: W. W. Norton & Company.

Neuhauser, J. (2001). *Supporting love: How love works in couple relationships: Bert Hellinger's work with couples.* Phoenix, AZ: Zeig, Tucker & Theisen.

Parker Hall, S. (2009). *Anger, rage and relationship: An empathic approach to anger management.* London, UK: Routledge.

Perquin, L. (2004) Issues of narcissism and omnipotence treated by the use of physical limits with a symbolic meaning in Pesso Boyden System Psychomotor. *European Psychotherapy,* 5: (pp 85-101). Retrieved October 7, 2014 from http://cip-medien. com/media/download_gallery/EP/2004/05_EP_Vol5_2004-%20 NarcissimPerquin.pdf

Pesso, A., Boyden-Pesso, D., & Cooper, D. E. (2013). *Sharing the practical wisdom: A compendium of PBSP concepts and insights.* Kindle.

Pesso, A., & Crandell, J. S. (1991). *Moving psychotherapy: Theory and application of Pesso system/psychomotor therapy.* Cambridge, MA: Brookline Books.

Pesso, A. (1984). *Presentations and Lectures on Pesso Boyden System Psychomotor 1984-2012.* Kindle.

Pesso, A. (2003). Cultivating the seeds of hope. In Jacoby, R., & Keinan, G. (Eds), *Between stress and hope: From a disease-centered to a health-centered perspective* (pp. 277-299). Westport, CT: Praeger.

Pesso, A. (2016). "Al Pesso Keynote address: German Humanistic Psychotherapy conference." *PBSP.* N.p., 27 Oct. 2014. Web. Retrieved on 10 Jan. 2016. http://pbsp.com/2015/01/13/al-pesso-keynote-address-german-humanistic-psychotherapy-congress-oct-27-2014

Max Planck Institute for Evolutionary Anthropology. (n.d.). *Experiments with altruism in children and chimps* [Video file]. Retrieved on 31 Dec. 2016 from https://www.youtube.com/watch?v=Z-eU5xZW7cU

Schnarch, D. (2011). *Intimacy & desire: Awaken the passion in your relationship.* New York: Beaufort Books.

Winek, J. L. (2010). Bowenian Family Therapy. In *Systemic family therapy: From theory to practice.* Thousand Oaks, CA: Sage.

References

Chapter 1

1. This process is called decentring: the therapist invites the couple to talk directly to one another, rather than 'through' the therapist. This was one of the methods I was taught at the Maudsley Hospital, during the two-year post-graduate training course entitled *Therapy With Couples*. Dr Crowe and Jane Ridley wrote the method up in their very clear and practical book, Crowe, M., & Ridley, J. (2008). *Therapy with Couples: A Behavioural-Systems Approach to Couple Relationship and Sexual Problems*. Chichester, UK: John Wiley & Sons.
2. Elisabeth Lloyd (2005) analysed 32 studies, conducted over 74 years, of the frequency of female orgasm during intercourse. When intercourse was "unassisted", that is not accompanied by stimulation of the clitoris, just a quarter of the women studied experienced orgasms, often or very often, during intercourse. Lloyd, E. A. (2005). *The case of the female orgasm: Bias in the science of evolution*. Cambridge, MA: Harvard University Press.
3. Schnarch says that "sexual relationships always consist of leftovers,": Schnarch, D. (2011). *Intimacy & desire: Awaken the passion in your relationship*. New York: Beaufort Books. p163.
4. Schnarch (1997) talks about the importance of learning to 'tolerate discomfort for growth' as one of the keys to sustaining a healthy passionate marriage. Schnarch, D. (2011). The Crucible Four Points of Balance | Crucible4Points.com. Retrieved October 7, 2014, from http://crucible4points.com/ crucible-four-points-balance
5. Eliot, George. (1900). *Middlemarch*. New York: H.M. Caldwell.
6. My NLP journey began in 1991. Most of my training was with PPD Learning, where I attended, amongst other workshops, six Master Practitioner programmes.

Chapter 2

1. As quoted in a review of *A Swinger of Birches* (1957) by Sydney Cox in *Vermont History*, Vol. 25 (1957), p355.
2. Hillman, J. (1996). *The soul's code: In search of character and calling*. New York: Random House.
3. I believe this was an expression first used by Harville Hendrix, best-selling author. Hendrix, H. (1988). *Getting the love you want: A guide for couples*. New York: H. Holt.

4.   Schnarch, D. (2011). *Intimacy & desire: Awaken the passion in your relationship*. New York: Beaufort Books. p376.
5.   Schnarch, D. M. (2002). *Resurrecting sex: Resolving sexual problems and rejuvenating your relationship*. New York: HarperCollins.
6.   Kerr, M., & Bowen, M. (1988). *Family Evaluation: An Approach Based on Bowen Theory.* London, UK: W. W. Norton & Company.
7.   Schnarch, D. M. (1997). *Passionate Marriage, Keeping Love and Intimacy Alive in Committed Relationships*. New York: W. W. Norton & Co.
8.   Gibran, K. (1952). *The Prophet*. New York: Knopf.

Chapter 3

1.   Schnarch, D. M. (1997). *Passionate Marriage, Keeping Love and Intimacy Alive in Committed Relationships*. New York: W. W. Norton & Co. p69.
2.   Ayot, W. (2011). Around, below, behind. *The inheritance*. Glastonbury: PS Avalon. p33.
3.   Parker Hall's book is a straightforward and helpful guide through the territory of anger, and rage. Parker Hall, S. (2009). *Anger, rage and relationship: An empathic approach to anger management*. London, UK: Routledge.
4.   ibid p2 and 90.
5.   There are further examples of PBSP in chapters 4 (using PBSP in a one-to-one context), and 5 (using PBSP in a group). In Chapter 6 I focus on a particular PBSP technique, called a Magical Marriage.
6.   Hudson-Allez, G. (2011). *Infant losses, adult searches: A neural and developmental perspective on psychopathology and sexual offending*. London: Karnac. Kindle loc677.
7.   Sanderson, C. (2006). *Counselling Adult Survivors of Child Sexual Abuse*. London, UK: J. Kingsley. p96.
8.   Gottman, J. M., & Silver, N. (1999). *The seven principles for making marriage work*. New York: Crown Publishers.
9.   Gottman, J. M. (1999). *The marriage clinic: A scientifically-based marital therapy.* New York, NY: W.W. Norton
10. https://en.wikipedia.org/wiki/Albert_Mehrabian

Chapter 4

1.   Pesso, A. (2013). Memory and consciousness: In the mind's eye, in the mind's body – Lecture at Nederlanse Vereigning voor Pesso psychotherapie conference, Netherlands, 2000. In A. Pesso (Author), *Presentations and lectures by Albert Pesso on Pesso Boyden System Psychomotor (1984-2012)* Kindle.

2. Ayot, W. (2003). Between dream and action. *Small things that matter*. London: Olivier Mythodrama Publishing. p48.
3. Al Pesso and his wife Diane Boyden co-founded the Pesso Boyden System Psychomotor in the 1960s. In 2012, Al Pesso was given a life-time achievement award by the United States Association for Body Psychotherapy (USABP) describing him as a "living master of body psychotherapy". *Pesso Boyden System Psychomotor | Lifetime Achievement Award*. (n.d.). Retrieved February 27, 2016, from http://pbsp.com/al-pesso/usabp-award
4. Faulkner, W., & Herman Finkelstein Collection (Library of Congress). (1951). *Requiem for a nun*. New York: Random House.
5. Al Pesso, personal communication.
6. The 'new memory shop' is a term that Al Pesso uses to sum up what PBSP has to offer. Al Pesso, personal communication.
7. In Sheila's one-to-one session, the Witness was brought in from the beginning, although to make it easier for the reader to follow, I only refer to the Witness part-way through the session.
8. Horacek, J., Pesso, A., Tintera, J., Vancura, M., Luck, L., Kobrle, L., Dockery, C. (2005). The effect of two sessions of PBSP Psychotherapy on brain activation in response to trauma-related stimuli: the pilot fMRI study in traumatized persons. *Psychiatrie (Czech Journal), 3*. This was a pilot study on seven traumatised individuals using functional magnetic resonance imaging before and after two PBSP structures.
9. Pesso, A. (n.d.). *Filling the holes in roles of the past with the right people at the right time: a new and surprising way to open the door to happiness in the present*. Retrieved September 20, 2015, from https://albertpesso.files.wordpress.com/2011/02/filling-the-holes.pdf
10. Pesso, A. (2013). Stages and screens: psychoanalysis revisited – grand rounds lecture. Boston University Medical School, Department of Psychiatry, Boston, MA, 1999. In Pesso, A. (Author), *Presentation & Lectures by Albert Pesso on Pesso Boyden System Psychomotor Therapy (1984-2012)*. Kindle.

Chapter 5

1. Pesso, A. (2013). Sexual abuse: lecture for studedag (study day) on sexual abuse held at Vrije Universiteit (Free University) in Amsterdam, Netherlands, 1988. In Pesso, A. (Author), *Presentations and lectures by Albert Pesso on Pesso Boyden System Psychomotor (1984-2012)*. Kindle.
2. Stockholm syndrome. (n.d.). Retrieved September 20, 2015, from https://en.wikipedia.org/wiki/Stockholm_syndrome

3. Cooper, D. (Ed.). (2013). *Sharing the practical wisdom: a compendium of PBSP concepts and insights based on structures and lectures conducted by Albert Pesso and Diane Boyden-Pesso from 1991 to 2004*. Kindle loc 217.
4. In PBSP the Loved-Aspect is a person who simply receives, but never moves or responds. When a response is needed, we use an Ideal Figure for that, in this case an Ideal Uncle, who can give love back, but who would always have held appropriate boundaries.
5. Pesso, Al. "Al Pesso Keynote address: German Humanistic Psychotherapy conference." *PBSP*. N.p., 27 Oct. 2014. Retrieved January 10, 2016, from http://pbsp.com/2015/01/13/al-pesso-keynote-address-german-humanistic-psychotherapy-congress-oct-27-2014/
6. Acharya, Sourya, and Samarth Shukla. (2012). Mirror Neurons: Enigma of the Metaphysical Modular Brain. *Journal of Natural Science, Biology, and Medicine* 3.2 (2012): 118–124. *PMC*. Retrieved January 17, 2016, from http://www.ncbi.nlm.nih.gov/pmc/articles/PMC3510904/
7. Pesso, A. (2013). Sexual Abuse: Lecture for the Study Day on Sexual Abuse held at the Vrije Universiteit (Free University) in Amsterdam, Netherlands, 1988. In A. Pesso (Author), *Presentation and Lectures by Albert Pesso on Pesso Boyden System Psychomotor (1984-2012)*. Kindle.
8. Perquin, L. (2004) Issues of narcissism and omnipotence treated by the use of physical limits with a symbolic meaning in Pesso Boyden System Psychomotor. *European Psychotherapy*, 5: 85-101.

Chapter 6

1. http://www.huffingtonpost.co.uk/2015/08/05/sex-survey-reveals-half-of-people-unhappy-with-sex-lives_n_7939598.html
2. International Society for Sexual Medicine. (n.d.). Erectile Dysfunction and Coronary Artery Disease | ISSM. Retrieved February 27, 2016, from http://www.issm.info/news/sex-health-headlines/erectile-dysfunction-and-coronary-artery-disease
3. I always ask clients with sexual problems to collect from the doctor's receptionist a printed copy of the results of all recent blood tests that have been taken. With this information I can check exactly what tests were undertaken, and look at the results to see if they are within the normal range, or on the 'edge' of the normal range. Any man with an erection problem should ask their doctor for a cardiovascular check. (see Appendix 4)

4. Such as the Rapport Ring Loading System from Owen Mumford, or the Easy Action Ring Loader from Osbon Erecaid. I warn Peter that when he is looking for these, he will find vacuum therapy systems advertised. These are pumps that can be used to draw blood into the penis. Peter will not need a pump, as these are for men who are completely unable to get an erection. In Peter's case, because he gets an erection, he just needs the applicator (loading system), and the ring, to hold the erection in place.

5. Cooper, D. (Ed.). (2013). *Sharing the practical wisdom: a compendium of PBSP concepts and insights based on structures and lectures conducted by Albert Pesso and Diane Boyden-Pesso from 1991 to 2004*. Kindle loc 2753.

6. This video is worth watching: Max Planck Institute for Evolutionary Anthropology. (n.d.). *Experiments with altruism in children and chimps* [Video file]. Retrieved December 31, 2015 from https://www.youtube.com/watch?v=Z-eU5xZW7cU

7. Pesso, A. (2013). Spirituality and Psychotherapy: The Becoming of the Soul in the Body. In A. Pesso (Author), *Presentation and Lectures by Albert Pesso on Pesso Boyden System Psychomotor (1984-2012)*. Kindle.

8. Teicher says "...diminished maternal attention also appears to be associated with lifelong decrease in production of the hormone oxytocin in the brain, and enhanced production of the stress hormone vasopressin. Recent research by Thomas Insel suggests that oxytocin is a critical factor in affiliative love and maintaining monogamous relationships. Both hormones may also help sexual response, with vasopressin enhancing sexual arousal and oxytocin triggering climax and release. By affecting these hormones, early neglect or abuse theoretically could predispose mammals to experience enhanced sexual arousal, diminished capacity for sexual fulfilment, and deficient commitment to a single partner... One consequence of childhood maltreatment is limbic irritability, which tends to produce dysphoria (chronic low-level unhappiness) aggression, and violence toward oneself or others." From Teicher, M.D. (2000). Wounds that time won't heal: The neurobiology of child abuse. Cerebrum: The Dana Forum on brain science, 2(4), 50-67.

9. Pesso, A. Retrieved February 27, 2016, from https://albertpesso.files.wordpress.com/2011/02/filling-the-holes.pdf

10. Pesso, A., 2007. Verbal communication, from notes taken during a training workshop in December 2007 in Richmond, Surrey. Al Pesso said, talking about systemic defences: "Their inability to complete will block happiness, because happiness means you've had the pleasure of completing things. Any time there is completion there is pleasure, but the completions that would happen [at the furthest extremes] are murder and rape, and in order not to let that happen, no happiness happens."
11. Pesso, A. (2013). Spirituality and Psychotherapy: The Becoming of the Soul in the Body. In A. Pesso (Author), *Presentation and Lectures by Albert Pesso on Pesso Boyden System Psychomotor (1984-2012)*. Kindle.

Appendices

1. Pesso Boyden System Psychomotor | Glossary of PBSP Terms. Retrieved September 21, 2014, from http://pbsp.com/about/glossary-of-pbsp-terms
2. Winek, J. L. (2010). Bowenian Family Therapy. In Systemic family therapy: From theory to practice. Thousand Oaks, CA: Sage.
3. Schnarch, D. (2011). Intimacy & desire: Awaken the passion in your relationship. New York: Beaufort Books. p85.
4. Pesso Boyden System Psychomotor | Glossary of PBSP Terms. Retrieved September 21 2014, from http://pbsp.com/about/glossary-of-pbsp-terms
5. Jacoby, R., & Keinan, G. (2003). Cultivating the Seeds of Hope. In Between stress and hope: From a disease-centered to a health-centered perspective (pp. 277-299). Westport, CT: Praeger.
6. Pesso Boyden System Psychomotor | Glossary of PBSP Terms. Retrieved September 21, 2014, from http://pbsp.com/about/glossary-of-pbsp-terms
7. Winek, J. L. (2010). Bowenian Family Therapy. In *Systemic family therapy: From theory to practice*. Thousand Oaks, CA: Sage.
8. Schnarch, D. M. (1997). *Passionate marriage: Love, sex, and intimacy in emotionally committed relationships*. New York: W.W. Norton. p115.
9. Pesso, A. (n.d.). Filling the holes in roles of the past with the right people at the right time: A new and surprising way to open the door to happiness in the present. Retrieved October 2, 2014, from http://albertpesso.files.wordpress.com/2011/02/filling-the-holes.pdf

10. Pesso, A., Boyden-Pesso, D., & Cooper, D. E. (2013). Sharing the practical wisdom: A compendium of PBSP concepts and insights. Kindle. loc 11184.
11. Pesso Boyden System Psychomotor | Glossary of PBSP Terms. Retrieved September 21, 2014, from http://pbsp.com/about/glossary-of-pbsp-terms
12. Pesso Boyden System Psychomotor | Glossary of PBSP Terms. Retrieved September 21, 2014, from_http://pbsp.com/about/glossary-of-pbsp-terms
13. Pesso, A. (n.d.). Filling the holes in roles of the past with the right people at the right time: A new and surprising way to open the door to happiness in the present. Retrieved October 2, 2014, from http://albertpesso.files.wordpress.com/2011/02/filling-the-holes.pdf
14. Weiss, Halko and Marlock, Gustl, editors, "The Externalized Realization of the Unconscious and the Corrective Experience" by Pesso, Albert in Handbook of Body-Psychotherapy / Handbuch der Körperpsychotherapie, Germany: Schattauer GmbH, 2006.
15. Grayson, J. (1999). Neuro-Linguistic Programming. In S. Palmer (Ed.), Introduction to Counselling and Psychotherapy: The Essential Guide (pp. 159-171). London: Sage Publications.
16. Pesso Boyden System Psychomotor | Glossary of PBSP Terms. Retrieved September 21, 2014, from http://pbsp.com/about/glossary-of-pbsp-terms
17. Pesso, A. (n.d.). Pesso Boyden System Psychomotor. Retrieved September 16, 2014, from http://pbsp.com
18. Pesso, A., Boyden-Pesso, D., & Cooper, D. E. (2013). Sharing the practical wisdom: A compendium of PBSP concepts and insights. Kindle. loc 5155.
19. Pesso Boyden System Psychomotor | PBSP placeholders, principles, possibility spheres, and stages & screens techniques modular training. (n.d.). Retrieved September 21, 2014, from http://pbsp.com/train/modular-training/pbsp-placeholders-principles-possibility-spheres-and-stages-screens-techniques-modular-training
20. Jacoby, R., & Keinan, G. (2003). Cultivating the Seeds of Hope. In Between stress and hope: From a disease-centered to a health-centered perspective (pp. 277-299). Westport, CT: Praeger.
21. Pesso Boyden System Psychomotor | Glossary of PBSP Terms. Retrieved September 21, 2014, from_http://pbsp.com/about/glossary-of-pbsp-terms
22. Weiss, Halko and Marlock, Gustl, editors, The Externalized Realization of the Unconscious and the Corrective Experience, by Pesso, A. in Handbook of Body-Psychotherapy / Handbuch der Körperpsychotherapie, Germany: Schattauer GmbH, 2006.

23. Pesso Boyden System Psychomotor | Glossary of PBSP Terms. Retrieved September 21, 2014, from http://pbsp.com/about/glossary-of-pbsp-terms

24. At the time of writing Juliet has ongoing PBSP groups in Bristol, London, Oxfordshire and two in Chepstow (one of which is specifically designed for those struggling with sexually inappropriate behaviour).

25. Shelley, T. (2009) *Medical aspects of commonly presented psychosexual problems*, Wessex SRT meeting, Romsey, Hampshire.

26. Clegg, M., Hallam-Jones, R. & Grayson, J. (Unpublished) *Female Sexual Dysfunction – Can we support a biased approach in the 21st century? – Introducing the Five Point Star Model.*

27. Schwartz, B., & Kloner, R. (n.d.). Cardiovascular Implications of Erectile Dysfunction. Retrieved September 16, 2014, from http://circ.ahajournals.org/content/123/21/e609.full

28. Between the period June 2013 and December 2015, of those at risk of sexual offending who contacted StopSO, 84% were self-referred, 12% were referred by a family member, 4% were referred by a probation officer, police, therapist, or other professional. 35% have not come to the attention of police or social services, 47% have been arrested, 18% are post-conviction. 217 clients in total have contacted StopSO asking for help.

About the Author

© Sian Trenberth

Juliet Grayson is an acclaimed psychotherapist, coach and teacher, specialising in working with couples and sexual problems. She also works with people who are terminally ill.

Juliet was one of the pioneers of Pesso Boyden System Psychomotor (PBSP) in the UK, and is amongst the first accredited UK trainers. She has been a UKCP registered, NLPtCA accredited, and COSRT accredited psychotherapist for more than twenty years. She is also a recognised supervisor for NLPtCA, COSRT and PBSP. This breadth and depth of experience has earned her the reputation as the 'therapist's therapist'.

She has developed a series of modular programmes for therapists, counsellors, and health professionals on sex and relationship issues, and on how to work with couples. She runs regular personal development workshops for the general public. She has a private practice in South Wales.

Juliet also has wide experience as an international corporate trainer and facilitator, and she is regularly invited to broadcast on issues of the day.

She is co-founder and chair of StopSO: Specialist Treatment Organisation for the Prevention of Sexual Offending.

She is a British Horse Society qualified instructor. She founded Barnfield Riding School which she ran for some fifteen years, during which time she set up Barnfield Riding for the Disabled.

Juliet's Twitter name sums up her values: **@HelpingYouBeYou**.

Made in the USA
Coppell, TX
07 September 2023

21340456R00150